Actively Adirondack

Reflections on Mountain Life
in the 21st Century

Also by Randy Lewis:

A North Country Quartet
Poetry by Alice Wolf Gilborn, Linda Batt,
Lorraine Wilson and Randy Lewis

Actively Adirondack

Reflections on Mountain Life
in the 21st Century

By Randy Lewis

Hungry Bear Publishing
Saranac Lake, New York

Actively Adirondack: Reflections on
Mountain Life in the 21st Century

Copyright © 2007 by Randy Lewis

First Printing

Hungry Bear Publishing
Saranac Lake, New York

Cover design by Andy Flynn
Layout and editing by Andy Flynn
Cover photo of Heron Marsh, Paul Smiths by Andy Flynn
Back cover photo of woods at Paul Smiths by Andy Flynn
Back cover photo of Randy Lewis by Colin Surprenant

Library of Congress Control Number: 2007921598

ISBN-13: 978-0-9754007-4-6
ISBN-10: 0-9754007-4-6

Printed in the United States of America
by McNaughton & Gunn, Saline, Mich.
on recycled paper (30% post consumer)

Book design by Andy Flynn

TO ORDER MORE BOOKS:
Books are available through the author, Randy Lewis,
581 Keese Mills Road, Paul Smiths, NY 12970,
e-mail: activelyadirondack@roadrunner.com

For everyone whose life is touched by these mountains

Contents

CONTENTS

Barnum Brook outlet at Heron Marsh, Paul Smiths

Foreword

Randy Lewis approached the Adirondacks somewhat hesitantly but with a firm grip on the knowledge of long, harsh winters with spectacular snows and cold, as possibly Thoreau approached the loneness of Walden Pond. Many people who come to settle in the mountains may not be aware of the rugged life they might be facing. Truly, the Adirondacks are paradise most of the twelve months of the year. summer, autumn, yes winter, and even mushy spring. Ms. Lewis was greeted with a fairyland winter and was certainly met by Jack Frost. In these essays, of a distinct charm, Ms. Lewis knows to put on another wool sweater, smile, and stack wood for the fire.

A reader can tell Ms. Lewis easily blended into the aura of the area, perhaps easier than Thoreau at Walden Pond, as she did not have Emerson, the Sage, to taunt her with a proposed failure.

The essays in this collection have wit, joy and information. Get out your hiking boots and walk beside her into the wilderness, pick a blueberry, or a wild herb, scent a marsh marigold, watch a woods creature scamper away. Ms. Lewis will help train your eye to see not just the wondrous views of rising snow covered peaks, but how to spot a princess pine, perhaps a magenta trillium, or an eagle high on a branch of a white pine.

Surely one of the most tantalizing, and informative, stories she tells is being 3,000 miles away on the West Coast and receiving a phone call that a distressed bear had gone into her home just behind Paul Smith's College. There is no need to tell of her anguish and the tale now. Read it for yourself, written by a woman who may not be a born Adirondacker, but one who has learned to nestle into its arms, its sights, its scents, its firs and furs. Relax and enjoy.

Maurice Kenny
in the Adirondacks
Autumn 2006

The author visiting Fish Creek campground, 1952

Preface

I did not come to these lonely mountains willingly. For a long time I did not even enjoy living in the Adirondacks. Feeling isolated and cold in winter, I missed a life containing real spring. I felt insulted by the dominance of biting insects. I wanted bookstores and coffee shops and people milling about, talking about their lives. I never would have chosen to settle in this place. But, as usual, life moves in mysterious ways.

Motivation for piecing together *Actively Adirondack* came about as an expression of Adirondack parenting, made fresh and sincere after my father died. Life is short. So I write about the full sense of this place for my sons, my unborn grandchildren, my friends, and my husband. I write these pieces for myself, so I don't lose small moments that have taught me things. And I write them for friends of the spirit, a spirit shared just by living here. I think of these words as casual talks I might have with someone on a walk in the woods, or while hanging out in my kitchen, having coffee. It's the juice of living in this precise place at this time in history.

In the middle of my years, I realized gifts this mountain existence offered piled up slowly, with quiet and peace. I've learned about patience offered by nature over time, repeated in forests and snowfalls and on the wings of birds. I've learned, as we all must, that this peace comes from within, sometimes with the help of a falling leaf or the cry of a loon.

I understand now, before I die, I want to keep a record of lessons this time and place have offered me. Mostly these essays began as journal entries, written from a chair by the side of the St. Regis River. Forgive me for saying "I" so often. Although I was just talking to myself in the beginning, I hope I've created a keepsake for those who follow me on the trails and roads of the Adirondacks. I want small truths I've discovered to resonate with people who actually live here, those who rarely stop to think about the enormity and uniqueness of what it takes to be a mountain resident.

I was lucky to be working as copy editor at the only daily newspaper in the Adirondack Park, the *Adirondack Daily Enterprise*, in the spring of 2000. I had great coworkers, and enjoyed going to work every day at the busiest place in town. Having always kept a journal, I'd written a nice essay about Mother's Day that I asked my editor, Andy Flynn, to read. He liked it and passed it on to the *Weekender* editor, who was then Bruce Young. The *Weekender* was the weekly arts and events section of the paper that most people held on to for its television section—meaning, it was a keeper. Bruce put the Mother's Day essay into the following week's *Weekender*, and my column, "Actively Adirondack," was born.

For three years I shared weekly glimpses of our Adirondack lives with readers of the *Weekender*, and the response was remarkable. *Actively Adirondack* is a small representation of that work, mostly published in earlier versions in the *Enterprise*, but some seen for the first time here.

Each chapter moves chronologically through the seasons, bringing a natural rhythm to our lives noticed with some help from a quiet observer.

These essays are not intended to be read as a novel, or in one sitting. They are meant to be savored in small doses, enjoyed with a turn of the great mandela, chapter by chapter, season by season. My eyes have seen the passing of years here in the mountains. I offer you, the reader, inside glimpses of this unique life, shared by the culture of mountain people everywhere.

It's not easy being a writer in this world of bugs, blizzards and frozen engines. But there are lessons to be learned everywhere, if you just take a moment to let them in. Sit on a rock, climb a mountain, walk on a trail. Be quiet and watch the world around you, a world cycling through its days and years without a single thought of you. That's where you'll figure out some of life's real stuff, clear as a bell.

Randy Lewis
Paul Smiths, N.Y.
October 2006

Long Pond, Paul Smiths

Acknowledgments

Thanks and appreciation go to many friends and supporters, especially my editor and publisher Andy Flynn. It takes a real Adirondacker to sense whether or not these words ring true. His wisdom and spirit propel me to try to get it right. In the process of looking back, I see a number of people whose impact has directly helped make this book possible. I wholeheartedly thank Bruce Young, Cathy Moore, Alan Steinberg, Phil Gallos, Peggy Lynn, Maurice Kenny, Stephanie Coyne DeGhett, Pat Willis, and the many dedicated members of my writing community, all for their belief in my words. I thank the village of Saranac Lake for offering me both the literal and figurative architecture of living in a mountain community. Every time I stepped foot in the Blue Moon Café, I was at home, the coffee was on, and the muffins were ready to melt in my mouth.

I thank the many readers who over the years have stopped me in the grocery store, or called me, or written kind cards when one essay or another moved them to speak. It's Adirondack people who make a difference. The creators of the annual Ice Palace for Winter Carnival, volunteers for the Adirondack Scenic Railroad, newspaper boys and girls, players on every school sports team, and clerks and waiters behind the doors on Main Street all make the spirit of this place soar, towering like the mountains that surround us.

I couldn't have accomplished even a fraction of the work these essays required without the help and support of my husband, Neil. He is wise and generous with his gift of time, is my partner in Adirondack activities, and is an excellent sounding board. My sons, too, offered support and hugs during the years this manuscript was being built. Families make life better, and people who live in the Adirondacks create a unique family of their own. I honor these people, and I am glad to be among them.

A requiem for two animal friends, written about in these essays: Cecil, my walking companion in "Walking in the woods with Cecil," and Spats, my eighteen-year-old black cat, from "Sunday Morning." Both long-time friends departed before the book went to press, but I am glad for their spirits being captured between these covers.

As I have been known to say, writing takes soul and time. Friends and fellow writers understand what it means to be required to take yourself away from people in order to write for them. Thank you for your patience, and your support.

I salute you all.

Snag at Black Pond outlet

photo by Colin Surprenant

Chapter 1

Adirondack Living:
Engaging With Place

The first "Actively Adirondack" essay,
opening a door to quiet observations of life
in these ancient mountains I call home.

Mother's Day

I am not a native Adirondacker. I was not born within the Blue Line. I am also not a visitor who enjoys summer vacations in these mountain villages and forests. As a child I frequently spent summers camping here with parents, grandparents and heavy canvas tents erected in the woods. Even back then it seemed a world away from reality.

Now I am considered a long-term resident of the Adirondacks, having lived here for more than thirty years. That doesn't hold water with the actual natives but does gain the attention of seasonal visitors.

Most natives will give you points if you bear children within the Blue Line, and I have done this. Most visitors to the Park will give you points if you actively participate in Adirondack activities, and I do. I live here. I have earned my points, and want to earn some more by sharing this extraordinary experience with you, the reader.

So, with those parameters clarified, I'll tell you about my Mother's Day morning, in the year 2000, in the wild Adirondack Mountains of northern New York.

I got up at 5 a.m., as usual. I laced up my running shoes, while the teakettle boiled. I fixed and drank a quick cup of tea, pulled on a sweatshirt, and walked out the door, before the blackflies woke up. It wasn't raining, and it wasn't dark and foreboding. The sun crept into view, lighting the tops of the very tallest trees on the horizon.

I drove a few miles down my road to the side entrance to the Adirondack Park Visitor Interpretive Center trails. Here I parked at the trailhead, sprayed my exposed skin with bug dope, put on a hat, grabbed my trekking poles, and got out of the car.

A quick check of the air showed no blackflies swarming yet, so I was very happy. A quick check of the melodies of the morning birds, and I detected no thrushes singing nearby, yet, either. Okay. I would find some of my favorite avian musicians in there, off the trails in these early spring woods.

As I began my morning trek, I noticed a few tiny wildflower blossoms. White trillium bloomed. Witch hobble blossoms decorated the woodland underbrush like tufts of white lace.

Poling step by step up hills and over streams made by the recent storms, I kept my eyes and mind peeled for the morning's lessons.

First message was from trillium, those lovely stars of spring forest undergrowth. This morning blooming trillium represented my three sons, its three leaves and three distinct petals on its flowers a gift to weary eyes after an always-too-long winter. Today they felt like my Mother's Day bouquet.

Trekking right along, I noticed the emergence of lady slipper leaves. Their flowers will come in a while when the trillium fades. For every thing there is a season. This always happens, year after year, with calm predictability—and the lesson is patience and promise. If you trust what you know, the reward of confirmation blesses you year after year.

I hiked quickly, energized by strong legs and even, hard breathing. Exercise at this time of day invigorates and rewards the soul. About halfway through the hike, I finally heard songs of thrushes overhead. For most of the spring and part of the summer, their flute-like melodies resonate deep in the woods, deep in my heart, and high in trees above me. These elusive birds are one of nature's most precious gifts, and their haunting music is free for the taking, early mornings, and at dusk, in special places in the forest. Today I was thankful for their music and feeling of preciousness it left me with.

I circled the pond and was startled by slow flapping of huge wings nearby. A raptor rose in slow motion, from a low spot on the shoreline into the sky overhead in front of the newly risen sun. A little blinded, I could not determine its features as much as its size. I stopped moving, gazing over this quiet pond as the mist rose off its still surface. The huge bird settled at the top of a nearby tree, adjusted its wings, then stared at me, yellow and black eyes gazing out of its white head. My next Mother's Day gift was to be in this quiet scrutiny by a bald eagle. I nodded and kept moving, a little nervous that black-flies would find me. I knew whatever the eagle meant to tell me would come in time.

I stopped at a bridge over the waterfalls, and raised my poles to the sky, thanking Mother Nature for her gifts. I saw the clear reflection of pointed trees on the water's calm surface, and wondered for a moment if my sons were reflections of me. Then the liquid surface was rippled by ducks swimming by, and the tidy reflections were jumbled and fluid in the wake. Hmm. I'd have to think about that.

I moved on. I bent over the edge of the pond to see if I was really there, in that other, reflective world. Sure enough, there I was, looking back at me, poles in hand, hat on head, smile on face.

Hustling quickly through the last mile, I listened to the birds while breathing deeply and evenly, thoughtful about being actively engaged with my personal piece of Adirondacks. Blackflies could come now that my hike was over. Just as I had that thought, they swarmed around my face and ears. But I won the race to have a morning hike in peace. I threw the poles into the car, got in and quickly slammed the door closed.

Got home, woke up the boys, and prepared for Mother's Day breakfast at the Blue Moon Café, a bustling world away from pond, eagle, and reflections in the morning mist, but really just a few miles down this mountain road.

Daily lessons can be learned from these unique villages and forests. Gifts of spirit are free for the taking, and not just on Mother's Day, and not just for me. That's what the eagle meant for me to tell you. And that's why I just did.

Refilling our senses

Whether or not we can relax and enjoy it, spring, which arrived back in March, is actually here. Since very few generalizations about weather can be cited this year, I'd call it a non-traditional spring, as many are.

Currently the Weather Channel has posted a winter weather advisory today, and outside my window, snow tumbles down.

More subtle gifts of an incoming spring are being provided by Mother Nature as the unmistakable evolution of a season rolls on.

My first observation this past week was a delicious addition of sound. Winter is gentle in this department. Forests are restfully quiet during most of our snowy time, with only an occasional blue jay or chickadee voice to balance with chattering red squirrels. Pure silence is often available, allowing us to hear the music of wind.

But now, bit by bit, we've watched the addition of first one, then another vocal species. Like liquid gold, their spring songs fill the skeletal forest air. Just this morning I listened to robins, chickadees, ravens, evening grosbeaks and blue jays. I watched juncos and purple finches hopping under birdfeeders, chirping.

A week ago, when our temperature was warmer, amphibians woke up. Wood frogs voiced their guttural croaking from nearby moist spots. Spring peepers had begun their chorus of cricket-like chirping, which here, next to several bodies of water, is an extremely obvious addition to a formerly quiet locale. I expect their small songs back when the air warms up again, tiny frogs waiting for their thermal cue.

Now I'm looking out at a small group of white-throated sparrows. Just a few days ago we were happily serenaded for the first time, from high atop a leafless tree, a long, pure white-throated song, pouring into the air above us after the long silences of winter.

Have you noticed that smells have returned? Melting snows moisturize the earth, and give us musty smells of mud and damp leaves, long quiet under snow. If you stand next to a river or pond, you can see that the shoreline has regained odors of moist earth and aquatic life, a little of that fishy smell we connect to being any spot where water meets land. Along with musty smells, the sound of water lapping at that edge of land comes back, reminding us of the liquid time, when ice does not hold court.

Along with the evolution of spring sounds and smells comes the addition of color. In winter we acclimate to soft invitations of white, with evergreens shouldering heavy white blankets on outstretched green limbs. Hardwood trunks, plainly brown and gray, stick out of the white scenery as markers.

Now brown earth has emerged between spring snows, and we see bright green blades of new grasses on lawns and in meadows.

Wherever there are people who garden, we witness the emergence of spring flowers, with bobbing yellow heads of daffodils and narcissus, and pastels of hyacinths gracing our vision. Timid harbingers of the new season, these flower bulbs were planted in a closing-in time, during autumn before the snow fell.

Returning songbird migrations also bring colors to view—red epaulets of red-winged blackbirds, ruddy red breasts of robins, yellows of goldfinches and cheerful reds of purple finches. All these beautiful feathered creatures stand out, cheering winter-weary eyes that gaze at early spring's twiggy forest landscapes.

Most subtle, but also most promising in the world of color, are buds on our trees and shrubs. While still leafless, forests are airy and light. The tiniest buds on all living limbs show their promise of sweetness with youthful color. Hints of royal reds, golden oranges, and yellow greens glow everywhere the spring light strikes. Sight of a hillside in pre-leaf condition is a whisper of color, a promise of what is to come, with an impressionist's careful wash of golds and greens to soothe our hungry eyes.

I never really mind these last few snowfalls every spring. For some of us, it may be the last time we ever see snow, with its riotous filling of the sky, and its quieting of the forest soul.

And for the rest of us?

Snow melts and we move on to the next season, which around here would be bug season. It's more definite than a promise of a long, sweet spring, that's for sure. But even those upcoming days of swatting and coexisting with flies have moments of pure pleasure. We just have to take note of where we are and smile. There's no winning some battles, after all.

Poles

Several years ago I was diagnosed with a slipped kneecap. I limped for a few weeks, then ended up in Doc's office.

"You'll have to rest this knee a bit, and get some physical therapy," began his advice

"But when can I run again?" I whined.

"Not for a while," said Doc. "We'll see how you are in a couple of weeks."

This was horrible news for me. I'm a religious runner and constant walker. Taking those options away from me was mind-boggling. So I tried physical therapy and enjoyed it. They gave me a brace to try to keep my wayward kneecap in place, and gave me exercises to keep the whole knee working. But I was suddenly in the world of the weak-kneed, and I didn't like it one bit.

After a while, I was informed that I may have some loose cartilage in that knee and might need surgery. After twenty years of running on only cement, I wasn't surprised. I did have a torn meniscus, and did have surgery to correct it. My carefree running days were put on indefinite hold.

Back in Doc's office, I grumbled about losing my legs' ability to keep me happily prancing through the woods. And, sensitive as he was, he had a suggestion that changed my life.

He pulled out his prescription pad, and began writing as he spoke.

"I've been hiking with these adjustable trekking poles for years. They are great. Light weight. And for mountain climbing, they can be adjusted to different heights for climbing and descending slopes. For people with sore joints, a lot of weight bearing can be assumed by the upper body when you use poles. Try it. See what you think."

He wrote down the brand name of the poles he used, and handed it to me. I was very curious, and slightly doubtful. But when I got home, I grabbed a pair of cross-country ski poles, and tried a short hike.

My first reaction was total joy at being back in the woods. My second was, "PHEW," the workout was much more vigorous than an ordinary hike. I was out of breath a lot sooner, and my arms were getting tired. I easily found a rhythm, however: one pole, reach, two fast steps, then the other pole, reach, two fast steps, left, right, it all fell into place. Hills did not hurt my knee as much, because part of my weight was supported by the poles and my arms.

I was amazed. I was grateful. Doc had come through again.

Over the ensuing months and years, I've become attached to these trekking poles. I received adjustable poles as a Christmas gift and now use them every day.

"Mommy, why is that lady skiing in the summer?" I often hear as I pass other hikers on the trails.

Or, after I've passed by, "Daddy, why does that lady go so fast with those poles?" asked a child. I'm usually out of earshot by the time parents come up with the answers, but I am aware that I am an unusual sight for children in the woods.

Adults say things like, "Bet you can't wait for the snow!" and I smile as I wing by, not wanting to discuss how much I dislike snow except on the rarest occasion.

Others say, "Looks like you're training" or "That seems like a good idea, having some protection," but I'm really just chugging along, not stopping to visit or explain myself to camera-laden tourists. Hiking poles make me feel strong. I think I am a four-legged animal, like a deer, able to scurry up slopes easily, and make it down with much less fear of stumbling. The tips of the poles dig into the earth, poking and grabbing the trail. My upper arms are strong as I grip the handles, at once pushing, lifting, and pulling me through the forgiving forest, which is happy to be adhered to by me and my sticks.

My knees hurt some days, but I am in that other group of people now, those knee-awares. I do not bemoan my fate. I have a gift, a positive that came of this. My trekking poles have given me back my hiking legs, have made my arms strong, and my stride long.

Ironically, until now the only other people I ever encountered with poles in the woods have been doctors. Maybe now a few more folks will give this action a try. It might bring you closer to the places you thought were not available because of sore knees or arthritis, or it might give you surprising upper body strength. It doesn't hurt to try, and may even make access to the forest available to you again. See you out there!

Rainwalk

Adirondack people of a certain type like the nice warm weather we had for the better part of the summer. Every one of those 90-degree days brought out smiling faces somewhere. Liking hot weather is quite possibly a genetic predisposition, and for some, a preference. Huge pools of humanity originally arose from hot weather places.

On the other hand, Adirondack people of a different sort do not like hot weather and rays of blistering sun beating on their exposed skin. This group includes people over the summer who found refuge in air-conditioned cars or grocery stores or malls, or who sought solace with other friends who seemed to be melting in long-lasting, hostile heat.

"We don't live here because of loving hot weather!" someone said to me. Someone else added, "Hasn't this been enough summer yet?" We wondered how drastic a change El Nino was bringing.

People generally have a type of weather they prefer, and when seasonal extremes tilt in the other direction, part of their comfort zone is disturbed. Ask me how I feel about our summer drought.

It's no secret that I love rain. Last night was the first in months where I could wake up and listen to soothing sounds of raindrops falling on trees outside my bedroom window. Mother Nature resumed her job of nurturing us, gently washing off dusty leaves, juicily soaking into the parched earth which welcomed every drop.

When I got up this morning the rain held on, and I saw glistening puddles in the road. Some of the lawn grass was greening up, after just a small amount of overnight refreshment. I was very happy. Giddy, in fact.

So, while it still welcomed me, I found myself walking in the woods in the rain. I noticed a wide spectrum of natural appreciation for this soaking after so long without. More birds were chattering, for starters. Mushrooms came up overnight. And leaves on the ground were shiny, colorful jewels.

I walked through the bog and noticed hundreds of tiny moths. Beautiful, small, white-winged creatures held their own against splats of liquid threatening them from the sky. Some were clinging to the underside of shrubs; some were in closed formation, under a flower or leaf. Their numbers were astounding, and I realized they were coming together for a reason. I walked right through their moment in the morning mist.

I thought about the big things, like life and death and the last time you see someone. I thought about people I cared about who are in hospitals, and wondered if I could absorb some of this fresh air for them, walking in the rain. I thought about some friends who were dying. Did they ever just want to turn their faces up to get rained upon one more time?

I thought about family, and connections, and being where you were needed when someone you love is lonely or afraid. I wondered if spirit was something you could strengthen, and if far away people knew when you were hoping and praying that they weren't in pain.

Looking up at some big old white pines, I wondered what makes certain trees live longer than others, and how come some have wise faces. What must it feel like to be so tall, so grand, and to reach to the sky for a shower after a few months without one? Those trees were mammoth and pulled powerfully on my heart. Something about perseverance was in the air around them. I could feel it.

I passed only one couple, dressed in raingear. I waved, and said, "Isn't this a wonderful day for a hike?" They looked at one another, like they hadn't thought of it like that, and kind of nodded.

The man said, "Well, at least there aren't any people out here, eh?" I'd been thinking about people who were with me in spirit on this walk. I'd been concentrating on listening to the raindrops on the treetops, and feeling how happy the forest was to have something to drink. But it was true, not many of us actually go out for walks in the rain.

We were gazing out over a foggy pond, mist rising, brilliant leaves beginning a slow emergence to grandeur. It was a lovely place to be. The air was warm, about 64 degrees, and the sky was full of rolling shades of gray.

Walking in the rain is one of those wondrous positive experiences for me. Today my face got wet, ferns splashed rain across my legs as I walked through them, and the canopy of trees overhead protected me from being directly soaked. Instead I was misted, rejuvenated, and refreshed. That one walk felt like swimming in air and made my genetic northern European stock very happy. All my ancestors come from a world of clouds and mist, so I truly belonged in the moment.

With environmental ebb and flow come big moments of appreciation, balanced with an occasional unsettledness when the world isn't the way you like it best. We need to be reminded at times that a hot sun is balanced with cool rain, and vice versa. Thoughts will come, if you let them. Whichever extreme we're in, it feels good to somebody, either way.

Forecast: Low early morning fog

Driving to work when the sun comes up has been breathtaking, all week long. Today I decided to go out and weave myself into that moment. Am I ever glad I did!

This particular week was quite challenging for me, since my goal is to always look at the bright side of life. Highs and lows abounded. I sent my kids off to school for the last time. I remembered thirteen years ago, that first time, those tiny boys. September always feels like a yellow school bus, falling leaves and sharpened pencils, and so it did, one last time.

I am still eating lettuce from my garden, and grinning because of it. Didn't get a single zucchini. One person was rude to me. Ten people were nice to me. The Saranac Lake soccer team won two games, and lost one. I paid some bills, and found more to pay. That's what the week was like. And early every morning, silver fog settled in nearby valleys while the sun rose over tops of ancient mountains, turning the world to gold.

So this morning I grabbed a sweatshirt and my hiking poles and took off for a four-mile jaunt into the morning fog to see if I could figure anything out.

The woods were soft to the eye, misty and kind. Red leaves on the trail were brilliant in the haze. I heard birds singing that I hadn't heard in weeks, almost as though I'd awakened them after a long slumber.

I came to a long boardwalk over a huge open expanse of bog. The sun was peeking up over the top of the fog; bog grasses were golden and whispered as I passed.

I could not see the other end of the boardwalk; it just vanished into the thick cloud 200 feet from my face. But above me, from left to right over the wooden walkway, was a huge fuzzy rainbow, distinct from the cottony fog.

I was awestruck. None of the sweating, hiking, and walking mattered. What mattered was the message here. I stopped and soaked up this wonderful gift. Blue jays squawked, red squirrels chattered, and a pair of ducks whistled by overhead. They all told me to take the first step, the step toward the unknown future, under the cottony rainbow, through the sunlit misty grasses. So I did.

I walked slowly. As I approached the middle, the place I came from faded, then disappeared. I couldn't see where I'd been, nor where I was going. All you really have is the here and now, what you see around you, and what you feel in your heart. I learned simply not to dwell in the past, that those old complaints, worries, and excuses should be allowed to disappear in this fog. I know that right now is the moment when you're under the rainbow, and you'd know it if you just looked up.

It seemed I was in a movie, and the musical soundtrack just kicked in, camera panning out to this beautiful natural scene surrounding me.

I kept trekking, covering a couple more miles before I found a place to sit and reflect by the water. I watched nature emerge from the slowly lifting ground cloud. First the tops of the closest trees emerged, then the veil was slowly pulled back. The center of those trees came into view next, then ground level, and finally trees further away, all poking their pointy tops out of puffy white fog.

A graceful transition, lifting fog is like improvement in vision when you finally get eyeglasses after needing them for awhile. You can find the world lining up much more clearly once the cloud starts to lift. Seeing clearly, understanding, it all comes together in nature, too. As I watched the fog dissipate, my own vision cleared enough to see a great blue heron, not too far away, stepping carefully through the marsh, pointedly keeping her eyes open for food. The first dragonflies began darting about, with papery wings offering a tiny crackling noise when they flew by.

I thanked Mother Nature for this gift of the golden lifting of fog, of acceptance of the unknown, and of patience. I learned lessons of emergence, blessings of rainbows, and the act of letting go. Not bad for a morning walk.

I stood up and began to walk away. When I looked back over my shoulder at the place I'd been sitting, I was shocked by the sudden appearance of a mountain. This huge piece of planet was closer to the bench than I'd remembered from earlier visits, extremely close, indeed. Speckled now with spots of red leaves in green forests on the shoulders of Jenkins Mountain, the entire image was doubled, reflected in the still pond.

I offered silent applause and singing in my heart.

That one scene proved to me that there is always something extra

photo by Randy Lewis

View from Harrietstown Hill

out there to learn, maybe just behind the next layer of lifting fog. That impressive mountain was there the whole time, in my uncertainty, on the foggy boardwalk, behind the rainbow, next to the golden marsh. My gait was energized by the mighty view I'd seen. We all might need to walk in some fog sometimes; answers to life's bigger questions just might need a little time to peek through to show you answers that were there all along.

Sunday morning

An old black cat sits on a rock by the side of the river, watching the water flow by. She lowers her head and drinks from the cool stream, and rests there, in soft, early morning sun.

No sounds of man are heard this morning. No phones ring. No cars or trucks race down the nearby road. There are no doors slamming, no radios blaring.

Chipmunks and squirrels dart among tree branches. Ripe apples splash into the river, tumbling from riverside apple trees as soon as their ripeness releases them.

Blue jays, with their scratchy songs, bring bird sounds to these treetops, and the color blue, bright, bright blue, comes alive amid the orange, red, gold and green canopy overhead on the wings of these jays.

A warm September breeze moves the air, reminding us of summer at the same time as reminding us of summer's end. On these warm winds leaves tumble, making a dry-paper noise as they hit other leaves on their way down to the earth. On these warm winds floats the sweet burr-noise made by nuthatches, seeking food in the bark of the trees. Tiny birds, they prepare to settle in for the upcoming winter, reminding us that true mountain residents are busy this time of year, with an innate urge to prepare for survival.

A kingfisher chortles madly, careening down the river, its big, handsome head and tough beak guiding the avian fisherman with skills of a stunt pilot.

Just a few moments ago, a mother black bear and her cub crossed the river over a fallen tree, moving slowly and easily in the kind, long-angled morning light. There was no fear or urgency in their stroll, just a couple of snouts pointed in the direction of home, and a natural bridge crossing the water, helping them get there.

Crows are congregating. Day by day, a watcher can see groups of these shiny black birds coming together, sitting high in the trees, or waddling by the side of the road. Without question, this is the time for bird family reunions; robins, sparrows, and great blue herons are coming together as the autumnal equinox approaches, getting ready for the certainty of what comes next, only weeks away.

photo by Randy Lewis

Black cat by the river

We humans add serious confusion to the easy rhythms of nature. Instead of the calm certainties of predictable seasonal patterns, people and their political issues add volatility, pressures, and fears to the natural equations. Wars are created. Daily terrorism becomes normal. Good people die unnecessarily every day. Rules created by people to manage society fairly are commonly broken redistricting, throwing away legitimately cast votes, and election recall are just a few that come to mind.

Some life that a watcher witnesses makes sense: falling leaves, tumbling apples, racing kingfishers, the gathering of crows. But there is some of the world that just does not make sense, pieces of life assembled by man like the destruction of buildings by suicide terrorists, the undoing of environmental protection laws to satisfy the urges of money and greed, and ever-increasing daily fears created by generations of global bullies. How does one small person create a meaningful balance?

People who live close to nature have recourse when society's uncertainties disturb the soul. Wisdom can be found. Go to a place where there are no hints of man. Go to the edge of the ocean, the top of a mountain, the surface of a quiet pond, or the banks of a gentle river. Listen for the sounds of a world untouched by humans. Watch the animals move through their days and seasons unperturbed by daily headlines. Watch leaves change colors, then tumble to the ground, as they have done for thousands and thousands of years.

Sense can be found in rhythms of nature, along with an inner peace that comes with it. Be the cat on the rock, watching the river flow by. The next time the headlines distract you, find an answer you can live with, right outside your door.

Celestial season

Part Two: Before we went to sleep last night, we set out clothes to wear very early in the morning. Long johns, hat, gloves, winter coat, insulated sweatshirt, all were ready. So were our lawn chairs.

The alarm went off at 4:30 a.m. We got up and dressed sleepily. We then took the lawn chairs outside and set them up in the middle of the road. The sky was black, with no moon and no clouds. Stars were out in abundance. With all those protective layers of clothes, I actually felt warm.

The heavens were alive with shooting stars. We'd been told that this year's Leonid meteor shower would be particularly dramatic, a once-in-a-lifetime event, so we were definitely up for viewing the show.

One disadvantage of mountain life is a lack of "big sky" that other geographical areas have. Any amount of sky unhampered by trees is good for this astronomical show, we decided. So why not the middle of the road?

With our faces turned skyward, we counted between 12 and 15 meteor streaks a minute, with about 60 to 75 degrees of visible sky. I guessed the number of streaks would have been higher if more sky were showing, but we were not the least bit disappointed by our view.

Long trails of light streaked from one side of heaven to the other. Sometimes two or three meteors were writing long brilliant lines across the dark sky at the same time. And, like watching a number of eager children all wanting my attention, my head and heart turned from one streaking spot to another while I grinned from ear to ear.

We moved the lawn chairs out of the road once, when a single car drove by, but we put them right back after it passed. I had a cup of hot tea and was very happy. Once I counted eighteen streaks in one minute. Then I just kept counting these gentle white stripes as they silently appeared, shot by, and vanished. I got to a hundred, then started over, in awe of the show.

Once it looked like Mother Nature was skipping stones in the pool of stars—three meteorites in a row, from south to north, pulsed through the darkness, light, dark, light, dark, light. I was humbled by the universe.

We went inside after about an hour. But after I'd warmed up, I couldn't help myself, and I went back out. The eastern sky was turning gray, and when I turned my face to the west, I counted twenty more slashes of light before going inside. I had already heard my first chickadee of the morning by then.

Part One: A few days earlier we'd gone to Plattsburgh on a shopping trip. Finding ourselves near Lake Champlain at dusk reminded me of a different magical phenomenon in the sky, at the opposite time of day. We drove a few miles north to Point au Roche state park just as the sky began to darken at about 4:30 in the afternoon.

We were treated to a living light show. A huge flock of snow geese came to the cove along the shore of Lake Champlain for their evening respite.

Numbering in the thousands, these magnificent white birds move through a darkening sky like silver sheets waving on a clothesline on a windy day. A massive group, they fly upward all together like white stars waving on an American flag. They will shift suddenly, immediately changing direction, and in formation, move sideways. Then thousands of white birds begin their circular descent to the water's surface, honking and chortling all the while.

Once down from the sky some geese waddle on sand, some walk on grass, but mostly they float along the shoreline like quacking balls of cotton, bright white against the steely gray surface of the water. When startled, they take off, lifting noisily from water to sky, again as a single mass of birds. From one edge of their group to the other edge, they rise as though a sheet was being lifted off a bed. It was hard to see any individual bird since the size of their flock made the group itself a majestic, shimmering being.

Up there in the sky, uncountable white birds in unison shifted suddenly in flight. Brief remaining daylight caught all their dark silver accented wings as they flew, becoming momentarily iridescent. Then the same thousands of bulky snow geese quickly changed directions to be all-white spots in the sky again. Over and over again in the heavens, twists and turns, an aerial ballet, white, then shiny, then white again. The viewer can be left breathless in its wake.

Our eyes, once drawn to the skies, are blessed with meteor showers on starry nights and graceful beauty of migrating snow geese during an autumn dusky moment. Displays like these are free glimpses of planetary grandeur, light in dark skies, and gifts for the grateful heart.

Remember to look up every once in a while. The sky is full of surprises.

Wheels

Vehicles play an important role in personal Adirondack culture. Adirondack towns are miles apart from one another, generally separated by expanses of forests, lakes and mountains. We need our wheels, our cars, vans and trucks. From the hours spent taxi-ing our children, to grocery shopping, to getting wood or to church on time, we need to be able to get from Gabriels to Lake Placid, or from McColloms to Lake Clear. On our way from Tupper Lake to Long Lake, or Wilmington to Jay, we will not meander through miles of Taco Bells, car dealerships, malls and tattoo parlors. Our towns are discrete, with a few noticeable homesteads between.

So, why mention cars? Because we personalize our vehicles as they become temporary dwellings for us. People engaged with the multitude of Adirondack activities house the artifacts of these lives in their cars.

Picking up the kids after school one day, it came to me. One of my sons opened the car door and had to move trekking poles, water bottle, bug dope, sunscreen, and granola bar in order to sit "shotgun." He grimaced as he tossed the stuff into the back, saying, "You know, I bet there aren't too many cars with all this stuff in them every day."

I began noticing the "stuff" we Adirondackers carry with us, to see if he was right. Paddlers carry canoes and kayaks on top of their cars during paddling season. Inside the car they have life jackets, paddles, bug dope and sunscreen. Canoe people sometimes leave their vessels on top of their cars while at work, or while grocery shopping. Just take a look at the various summer parking lots to verify this fact.

Runners generally carry a pair of running shoes, shorts, socks, and hat, water bottle, sunscreen, and bug dope. Some leave these items in a gym bag, some just toss them in the back seat or the car's trunk.

A cyclist will sometimes have a bike rack on her car, or have the bike in the back of the truck, or with the front wheel removed in the back of the van. In vehicles of bike people you will find a bike helmet, sunscreen, sometimes shoes and shorts, a water bottle, and maybe a fanny pack.

People who climb mountains during their available spare time might have hiking boots, hat, bug dope, sunscreen, socks, backpack, trail guide, and probably a water bottle available to them. In my climbing mode, I always have an extra T-shirt, granola bar, windbreaker, sweatshirt, and hiking poles, too.

Another version of the Adirondack driving-culture participant is the parent/taxi driver. I noticed two varieties of this species as I studied vehicles of people in my world. Drivers can be parents of younger children who require child safety seats. In those cars, you obviously find car seats, strapped in with seat belts. But you also find items parents need to entertain young Adirondack individuals strapped in against their natural energies. These items include: juice boxes, water bottles, cereal, granola bars, fruit, cookies, and the crumbs and spills that come with them; also books, toys, and blankets for rare non-eating moments.

When children get older, general all-purpose kid paraphernalia replaces car seats. Often this variety of kid stuff is related to the child's seasonal activity, such as hockey sticks and skates; basketballs and gym bags; baseball bats, balls, and cleats; fishing poles and tackle boxes; soccer balls, shin guards and cleats; lacrosse sticks, footballs, skis, snow and skateboards, book bags, and schoolwork; and of course, dirty uniforms.

Other items in these cars are related to food and drink. The same types of things we found in the little-kid taxi we find in the mid-sized-kid taxi, except now there will more likely be additional soda bottles, Gatorade, granola bars and fast-food wrappers.

Cars in this neck of the woods should all be equipped with some road-sense items. We need jumper cables, a spare tire and jack, a can of oil, ice scrapers, dry gas, a shovel, sunglasses, road map and a blanket. Some times of the year these items are more important than others. Whimsy suggests a driver carry a camera and some tapes or CDs, since you never know when you will see a beautiful sunset or when you will be miles from radio reception and need some rhythm and blues.

Personal wheeled vehicles help get us from home to our involvement, no matter how many miles between. Some kids' sporting events require a hundred miles of parental driving. Some mountains we want to climb are three counties away. We never know when one of our serendipitous moments will allow us a paddle or a run, but we are ready, with our portable transport, our homes-away-from-home on wheels, and our spirit of adventure. All you really need is to be ready, and willing, and you can make your own mountain story happen, any chance you get.

World of wonder

What exactly is a wonderland? The dictionary says it is "an imaginary place of delicate beauty or magical charm" or a place that "excites admiration or wonder."

Wonder causes us to feel surprise and curiosity. We say things like "this is amazing" or "wow, awesome" when we are in a wondrous moment. Since there is an element of newness to such an experience, younger folks, especially children, find wonder in their lives more frequently than most adults do. Since their experiences are all new, any given day of childhood is full of a possibility of wonder. Many adults marvel at that joyful aspect of childhood, and even envy it.

How many of us in the past few weeks have looked outside at the ever-accumulating snow and seen a shoveling job instead of feeling amazement at the beauty of inches of fresh-fallen whiteness? We tend to lose our sense of wonder somewhere as years go by. We grab our shovels to get the job done, so we can move on to another piece of business in our lives.

One day last week I was pushing snow from the driveway with our new sleigh-shovel. The job of moving snow has become suddenly much easier, no more twisting and lifting (with resultant sore back) whenever the snow falls. Smiling and rosy-cheeked, I was quite pleased with this wonderful new pushing tool.

I listened with pleasure to the surrounding quiet that fresh snow brings to a forest. I thought of "other-worldly" wonderlands portrayed in recent film series like *Harry Potter*, *Star Wars*, and *Lord of the Rings* and felt right at home here. I glanced upward and saw a large bird heading my way overhead. I thought, "A raven, so dark against the snow. How lovely."

But as the bird drew closer, and lower, I noticed an even flight, and an incredibly broad wingspan. When he was a few hundred feet away, I saw a clean white head, and I inhaled sharply.

The local eagle was gliding slowly, following the open river. I was standing directly below, staring up in hushed amazement. One reward for my afternoon of shoveling was being in the flight path of this wintering eagle.

I had to shake my head after he had passed by. Such a lucky per-

Kids enjoying a wonderland

photo by Randy Lewis

Building caves

son, I am, I thought. I think we all benefit from taking a moment from time to time to see amazing things in our wintry Adirondack world. I shovel off a path on my back porch all season long, so I can keep my birdfeeders full. Some winters, like this one we're in right now, lots of snow falls, day after day. That path stays close to the ground and its shoulders get higher and higher as days go by, creating an open tunnel.

I never stopped to think how much fun those tunnels would be if I were only three feet tall. Youngsters who come to visit see it immediately, and know it for what it is: magic. Recently I've gotten down on my knees to see the tunnel from their vantage point, and I discovered heaven, right in my backyard.

While shoveling that path at dusk last night, I startled a pair of black ducks, swimming in the moving water of the river below. They took off adeptly from the river's surface, directly into the snow-filled air right before my eyes. I stopped, hushed by the beauty of their dark wings and the sound of quiet honking, loud in this peaceful moment just before dark.

I've paid attention to wintering mammals, as well, in the recent days of heavy snow. They persevere in this chilly meteorology, looking for food in dependable spots, day after day. Red and gray squirrels and local white-tailed deer have their sensors tuned to my bird-feeding stations. Every day they migrate towards fresh seed which must appear like magic to them. When I'm home, looking out my windows, I quietly watch their moment of intersection with my day.

Today I watched a pair of gray squirrels barreling through the deep new snow so quickly, a pair of small tornados seemed to be headed my way, just like the hero in Road Runner cartoons. I couldn't actually see the squirrels en route but could see amazing swirls of snow as they raced bravely to my feeders, in spite of snowy obstacles. How heroic their journey! How determined they were to succeed.

A small family of deer poked around under the feeders and had me stymied for awhile. How did they always know when I put the feed out? Last night I discovered their trick. They've made a sleeping plot on an island in the river just behind my house. When my back door opens, all they have to do is glance up to see if I'm feeding the birds. If not, they curl up and go back to sleep. But if so, they hop up, cross the river, and nuzzle around for stray seeds. Their faces are furry, with snow crusted around their mouths. Their big black eyes are so earnest; I smile as they move into my world for these small quiet moments.

So what exactly is a wonderland? It can be something magical and imaginary, like in blockbuster movies we pay money to see. But it can also be something ordinary, lovely and amazing, right under our noses. It's up for us to decide.

Rhythms

I woke up, as I generally do on the weekends, to the sound of a pair of gray squirrels as they climbed from a large elm tree outside my bedroom window, down the south side of my house, using window casings and sills to grip as they scurried toward the "backyard diner" where I regularly feed birds. This pair travels this same route every day, I firmly believe. I only witness it on weekends, though, when I sleep past my normal 5 a.m. start-time. But I'd bet it happens every single day, with or without my attention.

These squirrels' route and daily ritual is a sample of rhythm in the natural world we live in. We all might be able to make these observations if we only had the time.

Daily natural rhythms are like a planetary heartbeat, keeping us moving along. I thought about the variety of rhythms of our lives, and the solace we can gain from their dependable patterns, far beyond what we ourselves control.

After one particularly stressful day last week, where I'd had very little control over an unfolding chain of troubling minor crises, I got home, put on my walking boots, and headed off to the woods. It was about 4:15 in the afternoon, still light enough to see and walk on my well-packed trail.

Chickadees were noisy, and in motion, gathering their last bites to eat before settling in for the night. I was comforted by their predictable behavior patterns, which I'd been watching for decades. Those little birds moved through the same day I did, yet did not carry worries with them into the night.

Being carefree is true for them every day, and it was a soothing thought. Overhead, a pair of ducks whistled by on a path they took every day, before settling in for their night. Natural rhythms offer impersonal and reassuring structure to life in the woods, and to us, the note-takers.

Other rhythms give structure to our days as well, some which we impose on ourselves. People who own dogs are often reminded to start their days by their canine friend needing to go out. Cat owners are accustomed to some form of feline nudge, when the cat knows her "person" should be up and moving around. How these animals know time is due to their adaptation to our patterning, living in our homes and lives with us.

People with young children notice a rhythm to their days, based on personal family patterns of waking, eating and sleeping. School buses come; day care centers open, and always, shoes must be tied first. Older folks create a pattern with medication schedules, diabetes sugar testing, having lunch at a senior center, or watching soap operas on television. We all have personal rituals giving order to our days.

Some of us check in at a local coffee shop every morning, and others pick up their newspaper at the same time and place every day. We know what time the UPS or FedEx trucks roll by, and when mail appears in our mailboxes.

Folks who live near an airport know from conditioning what time that first plane of the day will be circling for a landing. On rural back roads we know when the school bus goes by in the morning and when it returns in the afternoon. A gentle pattern of predictability makes us secure and defines us in our grid of interlocking humanity and nature.

In the flow of life in the woods, the first chickadees make their tiny voices heard in dawn's early light, and another day in the mountains begins, fresh and new. Chickadees are followed by blue jays, nuthatches, then squawking hordes of evening grosbeaks. Later come redpolls and woodpeckers, just as always, all winter long, year after year.

This morning the scurrying sound of quick-footed gray squirrels outside my window brought comfort to the beginning of a normal day in my neck of the woods. I got up, put the kettle on for tea, and then went outside to put out some extra seeds for them, as thanks for the rhythm they contribute to the days of my life. Lessons in reassurance come to me, thanks to those little gray harbingers of morning. Keep your eyes open for your own rhythms; they'll keep you connected to the flow of the pieces of your life, year after year.

Walking in the woods with Cecil

For a little while this week, I was privileged to have a great dog to hang out with. My neighbor, Keith, left his old female black lab named Cecil with our family for a few days while he went to the city.

Genuine poetry is the sight of an old Adirondack dog lying comfortably by a woodstove after a romp in the snow. A vision of peace, in fact.

She and I trekked back into the woods to sit for a while, observing the beauty of a snow-covered pond, with wisps of powder blowing across the open surface of ice. Cecil is a natural outdoors dog, sure of her footing in the six-inch-deep fluffy snow. I watched her as she discovered her own wonders on the hike, gleefully wagging her tail at a scent, or a set of tracks from a woods mammal.

Her fur is patchy, with thick layers showing that she's spent some hours outdoors, acclimating to the cold. She was entirely comfortable with the 18-degree temperature we found ourselves walking in today.

Several times I watched her nose take over as her sensory leader. She'd put her whole head under the snow in search of the scent, and come up grinning, her black face coated with white chunks of ice and powdery flakes of snow, like a little kid.

I was thrilled to be sharing my walk with another enthusiastic and quiet Adirondack entity I could relate to so well. We both are pros when it comes to prowling around the woods in these parts. Without words, we each know this communion. We both are drawn to the sound of moving water, places where rivers run over rocks, babbling all year round. We also notice the activities of other living things as we ramble under trees, each of us with a couple of noticeable gray hairs on our heads and a little arthritic hobble in our brisk walk.

We sat in a protected space for a bit, while Mother Nature blew snowflakes all around. Trees surrounding the pond made a faraway and deep whooshing sound in the wind. The high branches bowed and lifted in moving rivers of air up above.

From time to time, with a big gust, snow would tumble from a perch on a high, sudden-moving branch, cascading to the ground below.

I listened to amazing sounds the wind made and heard questions

photo by Colin Surprenant

Walking with Cecil

I swear were directed toward me. In those big, windy noises through the trees I heard the word "how" race directly to my ears.

Then I heard "who?" and "when?" and wondered if lessons were being offered to me by this gusting winter wind.

Cecil cocked her head from time to time, listening, but I bet the sounds she heard were totally different from mine. Our heads didn't look in the same directions at all. I heard the sounds of "now" and "soar" and "howl" as I let my mind wander in the wind. A tree cracked and I heard the word "call." A twig snapped and I heard the word "stick." And at the end, just before I left, I heard what sounded like "whisper" when the snow raced over the ice making tiny "s" sounds.

So many things to think about, as this winter settles in. "How" to manage a life in transition; "who" will I be as I make my way; "when" does one start to make difficult but necessary changes in order to give more meaning to an already good life?

The sound of the word "now" meant to me that I should be always living in the present; nature saying "look" and me saying "wow," a great touchstone when other parts of a life might seem con-tradictory.

Dusty snow spirits were rising from the pond's surface. Pale ladies dancing in white gossamer dresses, they twirled about, right before my eyes. They beckoned me to write it down, which I did in a

47

small notebook with a pen I kept in my parka pocket.

Great power emerged from these visions and sounds, simultaneously exciting and lovely. Gray and silver and white scenes were all made sharper by the happy presence of one pure black dog, biting snowbanks as she moved through our afternoon.

At dusk the sky turned a peachy color. Clouds became purple bands across an orange and pink background. As we headed home, we walked alongside a gurgling river whose silvery surface suddenly turned the same peach and purple color as the sky. The air was biting cold; my ears twinged and tingled, and my eyes watered.

We'd had whispering winds, dancing plumes of snow over ice, and orange waters flowing freely by: all gifts for the spirit. And here were me and Cecil, moving through it all, sharing life's adventure, side by side.

Community spirit

Being actively Adirondack, one participates with the environment here. Part of the Adirondack experience is the variety of different communities people belong to. Human communities make life bearable and rewarding when weather is brutal, when it is always night, or when being miles away from others creates an isolation threatening to break the spirit. Knowing other humans share these days and seasons gives us a sense of what it is like to be an Adirondack person. This is especially true when one lives away from town, streetlights and traffic, out where the trees make noise in the background, and rivers chatter all day and all night long.

I belong to several human communities, and each one is meaningful to me. As I list them, others who belong to them will recognize themselves. An early morning swimming community, the local basketball community, the been-divorced community, the Keese Mills community, the early-morning-trail-running community, the injured-knee community, the morning-coffee-at-Hyde's community, the mothering-of-teenagers community, the writing community, the teaching community, and more. We all have them, these places we belong, where our faces are known and someone might comfortably say hello to us.

In my neighborhood community, we run the spectrum of Adirondack involvement. We have people who were born in cities, who come from other countries, who work or went to school at Paul Smith's College, or knew someone who did. A few were born on this very road, like their parents before them.

We love to paddle, run, bike, hike, walk, make great food, fish, ski, snowshoe, brew beer, write, read, raise animals and children, grow food and flowers, shovel snow, play music, split wood, make a lot of money, or don't make a lot of money. It doesn't matter. What matters is that we all notice when a bear comes close to one of our homes. We keep our eyes open for strangers poking around where they don't belong. We know how close the lightning came, and if a plow took out a mailbox. We know when the river is running high or low, and when snapping turtles are laying their eggs.

Living far out in the woods, our vehicles are important. Most families have more than one, since you can't get stuck this far out without one at all. Community means that if anyone is going where you need to go, you can ask a favor. Just like family, someone will pick up supplies for you if you're stuck.

Our kids ride bikes on this road, from tricycles to training wheels, then to their first multiple gear bikes. In the blink of an eye, these young people then learn to drive. We all watch out for them, regardless of which parents they belong to. You might let them know they were going a little fast around the bend, if you see them, but you congratulate each of them as they earn licenses. They can finally get themselves around when that moment happens. We watch them suddenly taste the beginnings of leaving. The community goal is to get them all grown so they can make it safely anywhere they go.

Belonging somewhere is based on these daily relationships. Sometimes when you run regularly in the woods, you are actually in that woodland community, where trees, spiders and chipmunks are equal members with you. Birds sing for all the members. You are the same as a deer or a muskrat or a bullfrog in the big scheme of things.

I knew I had become a member of the inner forest community when, during my morning runs, I noticed that wild animals did not fear me. Birds that would hush for you, kept on singing for me. Deer lift their heads, then resume chewing without leaving their spots. Beavers continue their swimming and building, and red squirrels chatter, mouthing off at me to get out of there. They know I am one of them, a resident, belonging and understanding the messages.

So although I am not a native Adirondacker, I am a member of this forest community, both human and wooded. Because I walk the hills, run the roads, paddle the waters, and know my neighbors, I belong here. And when, like the birds and bears, I breathe in this wild air every single day, I know am not alone at all.

Waterfalls

Mountains, in their mass and majesty, rise from flatter, lower elevations to pointed or rounded peaks. Drama beckons the eyes of an appreciative human being, looking toward a mountain range from flatlands. Lower elevations frequently provide larger skies and a clear sense of distance. An observer gazes towards mighty walls of rock and earth tilted upward, pulling the eye toward a higher plane.

Mountain people live in that higher plane. Our cars move about on roads that wind through lower places between the higher hills and peaks. Often our roads follow rivers and streams, since Mother Nature offers water the path of least resistance every time. There are very few straight line grids in mountain country. Our views from everyday vistas peek around a mountain, over a pond, or between two hills, and are breathtaking. We can experience daily planetary grandeur if we only take time to acknowledge the bounty we are offered to see.

Living here, we fall into two categories: being lucky and being different. Our environment is raw, beautiful and pristine. Our lifestyle is sometimes harder than that of lowlanders, creating out of us a group with hardy survival skills and an earthy sense of community. As we all know, more trees than people live at these elevations. City folks have a hard time grasping that truth.

Mountain life takes place in a setting of constant change. Here are places where rivers run, filling with waters from mountain streams, moving downhill, always downhill. We see water in motion every single day, showing us constancy and direction. We live in an ever-evolving kaleidoscope of change.

Geologically, we have places where altitude changes from high to low in short distances, places of dynamic change. When rivers meander to those wondrous places, waterfalls are created. Powerful forces are at work showing the drama of geologic change, right before our eyes. Stand for a moment in front of a waterfall the next time you can and let it show you the incredible power of change. Being in the presence of waterfalls will fill your chest with awe, and make you humble.

Here in the Adirondacks many locations exist where one can easily visit waterfalls. Every river has them, to some degree or another. It's how all that flowing water gets down to the sea, after all.

photo by Randy Lewis

Hulls Falls in Keene

Adirondack people pretty much know where someone can find a waterfall, if you've been around long enough, and kept your eyes open. These exciting places have a way of beckoning a mountain person's soul. Here are a few:

• St. Regis Falls is one of those big, powerful places. Lots of water spills and foams in front of your eyes as you stand by the shore.

• The falls at Wilmington Notch seem to draw you to dizzying, crazy grandeur, tumbling and churning through its narrow passage downhill.

• Hulls Falls in Keene are dramatic bounces down rocky ledges. With surprising sharp geological drops, inviting and fast movement of water from up high to down low evolves, becoming a place where life is immediately quieter.

• Buttermilk Falls in Long Lake ripple, roll, and cascade from an upstream high to downstream low, filling the air with sounds of splashing water on slippery rocks, with constant motion and movement. Water is getting from up there to down here as quickly as possible, becoming a long, gentle lake where peaceful sunsets create serenity. Places like this are everywhere in the mountains where rivers run.

Waterfalls help us look at the art of change as nature shows it to

photo by Nathan Surprenant

West Branch of the Ausable River in Wilmington

us. We feel the power of the racing water; we see tumbling bubbles, splashes and spray, and hear the mighty roar of matter in motion. And as exciting as it is, we feel its ability to frighten us as well. Just like when confronted with major changes in our everyday lives, moving from one comfortable, ordinary spot to a distinctly different, unusual one, a trembling in the belly lets us know the power of personal change is at hand.

It helps to remember, though, that even the mightiest river slows down again after the waterfalls. It's going where it needs to go to get to where it needs to be. A calm certainty rings with that truth, an evolutionary correctness that can teach us something. Here's to the gifts and lessons of waterfalls, and all the places we find them in our mountain life.

photo by Colin Surprenant

Chapter 2

Life Around Here:
Saranac Lake and Environs

Once, in a Blue Moon

Outside wind is blowing the snow around. Snowbanks are much higher than they were just yesterday morning; I'd guess now they're about two or three feet high.

Inside, the Christmas tree stands by one of the front windows; Santa sits in the other. People gather at small tables, rock-and-roll music is playing over the loudspeakers, fresh coffee is brewing, and eggs are sizzling on the grill.

A few families are eating breakfast, winter jackets hanging on the backs of their chairs, kids munching on bagels and pancakes, parents gobbling their eggs before the kids get unruly. It is New Year's Eve morning at the Blue Moon Café in Saranac Lake, New York.

People coming in from outside stomp snow off their boots, and brush snow off their hats. They readily gravitate towards the coffee thermoses and cups. It is a perfect moment during the final day of the year 2000. Rosy cheeks, steaming coffee, and companionship.

The walls of this eatery offer displays of original artwork hanging for all to appreciate. This includes local artist Tim Fortune's community mosaic, with its hundreds of little faces smiling out at the assembled customers. Several tables are surrounded with folks reading newspapers; it is Sunday morning after all. I see a *New York Times*, *Adirondack Daily Enterprise*, *Albany Times Union*, *Daily News* and a Plattsburgh *Press-Republican* being read right now. Many people have left their colorful winter hats on, and several kids run with their mini-Sorels on, stomping about cheerfully, dressed for the season, snow pants and all.

I'm having a huge, delicious cranberry-peach muffin, with butter melting inside. My husband is eating a salmon-filled bagel. We're talking about the girls basketball team winning the high school holiday tournament and chatting with townspeople as they walk by our table. I wanted to spend an hour here this morning as a marker, because I was here last year on December 31. I'd bought cards to send to members of my family, and postcards of Saranac Lake to insert in each card. I sat quietly that Saturday morning, drinking coffee and writing a few words to each of my loved ones. I had my stamps ready. I was going to send them each a card from one century to the next.

Blue Moon Café, Main Street, Saranac Lake

While not as momentous as it felt at the time, it was the least I could do to pay homage to the big good-bye to the 1900s, the century that had begun with horses and buggies and ended with space travel. I had already walked around downtown, taking snapshots of the angle of the sun over Broadway, up Main Street, and where the river cuts through town. I wanted to remember 1999 as much as possible. I was a little afraid of what might come next.

I had enjoyed a decent percentage of my time in that century, and knew my kids would be spending a lot more time in the next one. So a small memento was called for, one they might hold on to, to pass along to their children, who might do the same thing when the century turned again, a hundred short years from now. I put the postcard from Saranac Lake in the card so they would remember exactly where they lived when the big ball dropped, and the fact that someone at that time truly loved them. I even sent a card to myself, got to the post office in time, and mailed the souvenirs through time and space.

ZIP! One year from that day, to today. Amazingly, it was a fast year, full to overflowing with good people, hard times and good times, changes and magic. People inside the Blue Moon might be different, but they might not. The coffee? Maybe the same. Gray hairs? Maybe a couple more.

The wind picking up outside symbolizes the changes, a sweeping by of time and weather. Blowing snows are both harsh and white, unforgiving and cold. But inside the café, it is warm and friendly. People assemble, then separate, and move on to their different days. One guy walked in, brushing snow off his shoulders, and said to the people waiting at his table, "They're all out of sleds at Ames. What should we do?" Everyone chatted, coming up with some way to play outdoors today, to end this year with some winter fun.

When we got home, we shoveled snow. We shoveled a lot of snow, laughing, and getting rosy cheeked. We got some of the kids to help us, and got into the familiar rhythms that veteran snow-shovelers seem to have. It wasn't brutally cold and shoveling itself was sweet, fun, and symbolic. We pushed it aside, carving out a manageable niche in our winter wonderland. We lifted, hoisted, pushed, and threw it by mounds, building banks and pathways, warming ourselves as we always do.

Then we came inside, to warm our noses in the steam of hot tea or cocoa, like Blue Moon customers do in town. There is work

photo by Randy Lewis

Saranac Lake in the last moments of the 20th century—Dec. 31, 1999

involved with living here in the mountains, and there is reward.

Passage from one year to the next is a fitting time to respect the work, and recognize the rewards in the heart of the cold dark time, in the heart of the Adirondacks. Sit back by the wood stove, and let the winds blow. They always will, you know.

Another time, same place

While this second wave of long-term frigid weather bears down on us this year, the memorable winter of '03, I notice that human life in the Adirondacks goes on. Maybe it's moving a bit more slowly than usual, but life here does keep going. We all move about our days, watching chimney smoke rising in the early mornings from homes and buildings in the village. An awesome beauty fills the high peaks, which look majestic and white, and even colder, if imaginable, than where we stand gazing.

Someone recently mentioned the winter of 1979 as the last time it was this cold for this long. I remember it well. I swore I'd never forget it.

I was living in a small, uninsulated cabin near the Saranac River that winter. The only heat was provided by a room-sized propane space heater, which we'd gather around, day after frigid day. We sat in rocking chairs, bundled with blankets and long johns and more than one pair of socks. We drank tea, read books, and waited to go to sleep just to get up the next day. We hoped bleakly for a break in the cold. We covered the windows with blankets that year, too. The glass was completely ice-covered behind all that wool.

We lived downstairs in the three-room (two upstairs, one down) cabin. If you went upstairs and exhaled, you could make it snow indoors. Houseplants froze. Water in the cats' dishes froze. We left the water on in the sinks, dripping quietly, hoping the pipes wouldn't freeze. Not unlike this winter, the cold snap just lasted and lasted, week after week. It was a bad movie. Bad, but very beautiful. Those clear, cold days were bright, blue-skied wonders.

Sometimes these unnaturally cold times are spirit-busters. But sometimes they build spirit instead. I remember more than once that year, gathering in one cold cabin or another with friends, eating hot stew or chili, laughing at the insanity of living somewhere so arctic. Actually, the humor was making the choice to live here, when there was a whole other world out there, not so cold. We still remembered that other world; we hadn't been here in the woods all that long yet.

But that fact was our bond. We'd all chosen to live here. Our talk was about long johns, socks, and ways to start cars, nearly all models which seemed to rebel at a constant temperature below ten below. Jumper cables, block heaters, window quilts, heat tape, and wood-stoves were topics we'd share. We were the up-and-coming generation of Adirondackers, learning our trade firsthand.

I remember one day back during that cold spell of '79 when neither car would start. While the sun shone so brightly, the icy air was so brittle, you'd think it would break if you exhaled. In order to get to work, I had to hitchhike from Bloomingdale (where the cabin was) to Saranac Lake (where the bookshop I worked at was located). The temperature rose to minus fifteen by nine in the morning, so I headed out. The view of Moose Mountain was beautiful, its scar white and crystalline.

As soon as a passing motorist saw me, with my mittened hand outstretched, thumb begging for a ride, she pulled over, and offered me a ride. I got in, and immediately began defrosting.

Why, here was an automobile that worked! And it had heat! And a cheerful driver! Suddenly the world was not such a forbidding place. The kindness of strangers pulled me through the blues again.

When I got to work, the key opened the door. Sure enough, inside the bookshop, heat pulsed from the radiators. Sunlight poured in the tall Main Street windows, onto a nice green carpet. Hot coffee was available nearby at Alice's Restaurant, and the newspapers arrived from other towns, like Plattsburgh, Albany, and New York City, proving that the outside world kept turning. Life was moving on, regardless of how still the arctic air was outside the window.

Customers stopped in for their papers, or to pick up a book they'd ordered. The store wasn't very busy, but there was village life, and the neighborly smiles that went along with it. We all wore our Winter Carnival buttons and our Sorels, and were glad to know we were a community of fellow winter survivors.

It was a painfully cold winter, definitely. But spring did come. I swore I'd never forget that fact, either.

We find warmth during these rough times. We seek it and smile when it finds us. Some miserable times threatened the spirit back in the long cold snap of '79. I had no idea how cold a house could get, or how little fun it was to live where it froze the windows solid. But I'll never forget how beautiful it was, either, how raw and clear.

This year's cold has also been harsh for many of us, with our cranky cars, stuffy noses, long coughs, dwindling wood supplies and rising gas prices. But the world is turning, and it revolves in its orbit,

photo by Colin Surprenant

Running in the snow

just as it always does. In a month we'll have an equinox, then daylight begins to win the numbers race. Extremely cold years are followed by not-so-cold years, but they keep rolling by, either way.

Enjoy the character development of surviving one of the most memorably cold Adirondack winters on record. Especially enjoy the smiles we share with one another. Rosy cheeked, scarf-and-hat-enveloped smiles warm the community, no matter how cold the air.

New angle of light

Something about the angle of light from the sun now in late afternoon reminds me of spring. I can't put my finger on it, but I feel it all the same. That cool breezy feeling is accompanied by icicles dripping, freeing up frozen water, making it liquid again.

It seems irrational to think about spring in the heart of winter, but something about lengthening days tells us something is changing, very slowly, but dependably. These next few months make up the time every year which can try an Adirondacker's soul. When there are planetary clues, like longer angles of light and longer hours of daylight to indicate spring might be coming, some part of us begins to yearn for that season to be here. Yet spring's actual arrival is a long way off, as residents patiently (or not) know.

Saranac Lake's Winter Carnival is over. Basketball and hockey seasons are winding down, with only playoff teams left suiting up for games. Back roads are rutted with old ice ridges, and a daily slog of snow. Our cars are all pretty dirty, regularly sprayed with mud puddle water and slush. Now is a down time.

We have to remember that winter this year began later than usual. In fact, forests and fields have only really been snow covered since mid-December. We've been lucky to have a minimum of hazardous driving days. This year, as entertainment for sports enthusiasts, we also have local Olympians to watch on TV or read about in the paper. Snow is still falling regularly, bringing a fresh clean slate to those who love to ski, snowboard and snowshoe. True peace is available in the forest, white, calm and quiet.

As long as we find a late-winter niche for ourselves, weeks roll by, and "the back of winter" is broken. Meteorologically, the end of the forward thrust, or high tide, of winter is February 28, according to the mellow prognosticator on the Weather Channel.

So, I've decided to make the most of this period of lingering calm. After recently receiving a list of "what I've learned" items written by national columnist Andy Rooney, I'll follow his lead and make a list of a few winter wisdoms I've picked up over the years.

Here are some winter tidbits:

• After a late afternoon ski or snowshoe, sometimes a steamy

photo by Colin Surprenant

St. Regis River, Brighton

cup of hot cocoa with a shot of peppermint schnapps is the most perfect reward.

• Feeding birds outside connects you to their environment. Pleasures of watching these tiny living co-habitors are immeasurable.

• Going for a walk every day rewards you in many ways. One, you get to see the lovely world we live in, close up. Two, you get to breathe fresh clean air. And three, you create endorphins, which are "happy" chemicals in your body, known for improving dispositions. Plus, walking builds fitness.

• Snow fleas are harbingers of late winter, more than early spring. They are here now, black hopping flecks on nearby snow-banks.

• Of all the beauties in the world, the sight of the sparkling dia-monds of fresh snow in bright sunlight is right up there with the best of them.

• As bundled up as we get, we know most Adirondack winter weather is totally endurable, and even enjoyable, if you just dress properly for it.

• Binoculars bring excitement to your brain, especially when viewing wildlife. I've been able to watch squirrels stuffing seeds in their mouths with their tiny hand-like paws; mother deer nuzzling their young; and the bright white feathered head of a bald eagle flying

Black Pond outlet

overhead, all seen up close through my trusty binoculars.

- Planning a garden is a wonderful way to pass time during these lingering days of winter.

- Flocks of evening grosbeaks make an enormous amount of squawking noise when they gather in trees outside my bedroom window. This is their song, their mighty song. It reminds us that we share the forests with small gentle creatures who talk a lot.

- Kids generally enjoy playing in snow. Their smiling rosy-cheeked faces confirm this. We should learn something from them about access to joy.

- Spending too much time looking back at what used to be, or might have been, doesn't help you enjoy today, and the gifts it offers. This is especially true during this time of year.

- Be kind to your skin in winter. Cold air dries it out, and dry heat dries it out, so keep it moisturized.

- When roads are hazardous, SLOW DOWN. REALLY SLOW DOWN.

- Carry a little notebook with you. Write things down as they occur to you. Make connections, and don't lose them. Honor your ideas. You'll find you have a lot more of them than you think.

- Also, honor your friendships. They are sustenance for your soul. Just like watering your plants, give them attention. Tell just one person that you appreciate him or her, and see how much sunshine your words bring back to you both.

Filling in the empty spaces

Some weeks surprise us with the events they fill up with. This week I watched empty branches on our spring trees change from bursting buds to tiny leaf sprouts. This emergence brought dusty-hued greens and golds to view on the hillsides, filling in with color where we'd adjusted over the months to a winter of grays and browns.

Millions of tiny leaves are here. While these leaves take shape and grow to the full sizes their trees require for photosynthesis, we are witness to their growth and persistence in the world. Every day there is less open space in the forest. We see more leafy displays, hear more rustling in the wind, and feel more shade than the day before.

This time is the opposite of what we experience in autumn, when we admire the glorious colors each of these small green leaves will take on before tumbling to the ground. In the springtime turn of the great mandela, what goes away every October simply returns as it promised.

A similar phenomenon occurs in my house, when the kids return from a year away at college bringing home boxes of acquired "stuff," filling in a winter's worth of empty space. Like out in the woods, with unfurling ferns and blossoming trillium, a new busyness is here. New alarm clocks are ringing, new schedules are posted, more laundry is created, and much like the returning singing birds in outside trees, new music returns to the rooms inside our home. "Bustling" becomes an adjective of choice when responding to queries of "howzitgoin?"

Along with the visual concept of millions of returning leaves on Adirondack trees comes the often-timid confrontation of a small number of Adirondack humans with millions of tiny blackflies. These flying mountain inhabitants have just now come alive, hungry for our blood.

As usual, this massive return seems to happen in a single day. One day you can be gardening or hiking, or sitting outside in a lawn chair reading the paper and having a cup of coffee. The next day, your exposed skin is a magnet for these thirsty little insects. They swarm around us all: around our hands, ankles, arms, legs, faces and necks.

We do whatever it is we've learned to do at this time of year. Some slather on bug dope and cover up with protective clothing, and just continue with their plans. Others stay indoors until the worst is passed, generally in a couple weeks. Others bat and swing at the clouds of teeny insects, and move quickly to get away. And some just don't care. They go out, get bit, smack a few they can catch on their skin, and let the others have their way.

I do a combination of things. I've learned to garden in the rain, when the blackflies are less assertive. I walk in the rain, too. It feels wonderful this time of year. I go for runs very early in the morning, before the insects are fully aware there is life out there. I also take frequent road trips to Plattsburgh and Burlington, where the flies are not as all-pervasive as they are here. And sometimes I, too, slather on bug dope and cover up, finding I can win small battles in the bigger war with the hordes of "flying teeth."

For outdoor activities, early morning runs, canoeing and kayaking, and bicycle riding are all winners when facing these bugs. Canoeing and kayaking can usually be enjoyed, moving fast and away from the shoreline, by happy paddlers, unworried about bug bites. Same with folks on bicycles who are cheerfully pedaling down the road, way too fast for a blackfly party to consider a chase. And if it's walking you want, the hike around Mirror Lake in Lake Placid is well lit at night, when there are no blackflies awake.

We are very lucky to have so many recreational choices at this time of year. Look around at the children playing outside; they're not letting these bugs bother them, they're just happy it's nice out! We can choose to grin as our mettle is tested, year after year.

On top of these outdoor ideas, there are also a number of fun indoor options that look tantalizing, especially after an afternoon of swatting at flies outside.

Some current examples of protected indoor fun are at the area art galleries with spring shows opening. The Adirondack art chairs exhibition starts this week; musical performances are plentiful at the local schools; and regional theater performances like *The Guide*, performed at the Lake Placid Center for the Arts, and *Charlotte's Web*, performed at Pendragon Theatre, are in progress. Great talent is in our midst for your viewing enjoyment.

The Discover Jazz Festival is coming to Burlington next week, and at the same time, the Lake Placid Film Forum returns to Lake Placid, and brings world-class filmmakers, actors, and critics together for workshops, discussions, and the showing of dozens of first-run independent films for film buffs everywhere in the area.

We can enjoy one another's company, have a good laugh, and have some great cultural experiences during blackfly season.

So of course we'll mow our lawns, plant our gardens, and put screens in our windows. We'll fill in our days with satisfying activities of late spring, in the niche we've created for ourselves in our mountain communities. Side by side with pollen and blackflies, and soon, mosquitoes, we grab our running shoes, paddles and bikes for a whirl in the fresh air, made fresher by new growing leaves, and the spirit of endurance that makes us proud.

And if we're really smart, we'll go to a play, or see some innovative independent films, or drive over to Burlington to listen to some jazz, permission granted to avoid being chewed alive by the blackflies at home. Life is grand, here in the mountains. It fills in all the empty spaces, and makes us rich with possibility.

Digging change

In the short time known as spring, many Adirondackers actively engage in earthy activities like gardening. Some people start seeds indoors when snow is still abundant outside their windows. Others wait until they can work the soil with their hands and hand tools. We buy seeds and spring bulbs, studying planting times for this area carefully. We look for plants in nurseries, greenhouses and garden centers, all primed for enticing us to participate in our short northern gardening season.

I generally buy more plants and seeds than I ought to, going back one more time for red geraniums or purple-and-white petunias for the back porch. My heart sees summer's flowering season stretching long into October, and color is absolutely necessary during this time. After all, it is so barren for so long, with drab grays and white for most of the year, that balance is required.

Spring planting and earth work usually follows Mother Nature's contribution of flowering trees and shrubs. Apple blossoms' light pinks and whites have just blown away, scattering petals everywhere, a gentle confetti celebration of promise after the ball. Lilacs are gracing our nostrils with a sweet smell that always says "lavender" and makes us smile. This is digging time.

The Tri-Lakes area this year is also digging in, becoming actively involved with the earth on a larger scale. As observers, we are seeing dirt in places we don't usually expect it. Right in the middle of Saranac Lake, Newberry's parking lot is not a parking lot right now. Shifting and changing, the brown dirt is seeing the sky for the first time in many years. Larger machines than our gardening tools were needed here, but improving appearances was the spring goal, just the same.

On Lake Colby Road, the front entrance to the Adirondack Medical Center is also being reworked at the earthen level. Grass was dug up, cement removed. Huge mounds of rich brown dirt have been moved and moved again, familiar parking areas gone, new ones created.

And out at Paul Smiths, the college is creating a new entrance to the school. Old over-paved roads were dug up and earth bulldozed into new hills, which now are piles of dark rich earth.

Entering Lake Placid from the west, we see a huge expanse of brown earth acreage just before town, ready for a new building project, and on the other side of the road, many piles of dirt, looking ready for adventure.

Everywhere it seems that spring is the time for anticipating positive changes, planning and engaging with the earth. While we ordinary humans plant seeds, bulbs, and plants in rich, brown soil, larger project engineers will be putting down sod and planting trees around the new spaces they have created.

Change is generally uncomfortable, though. Most of us know this as we pass through life's marking spots, for example, when we are a part of childbirth, death of a loved one, marriage, divorce, job loss, financial disaster, or major moves. Change implies that something that used to be will be gone, and something new and less familiar will be in its place. Transition from one to the other makes some people uneasy, especially when they have no control over the process.

Let's remember that in order to grow, we must accept and welcome change. From weeding out dead plants and turning over the soil in anticipation of planting a garden, to digging up roads and old parking lots to make better sites, spring is a time to roll up your sleeves, take a deep breath, and dig in. Change is normal and invigorating. When you participate in it actively, you can be rewarded, and you yourself can grow. It is all happening now, right before our eyes.

So I'm off to greenhouses to look for geraniums, petunias, zinnias and cosmos, and maybe a new hand spade. How about you?

Spring cleaning

Prelude: The river out back is full and vigorous, racing earnestly toward the St. Lawrence and eventually to the Atlantic Ocean. It knows its direction, spills over its banks, and makes white-capped ripples when it catches on rocks and beaver dams as it races by. Full of water of diminishing remaining snows, it keeps going, always headed downhill. This wet spring abundance is a release from the confines of winter; it is a happy, healthy busyness, and has occurred for eons, ever since the ice age receded, and long before we were nestled in pockets of civilization here in the north woods.

My town is holding a town-wide spring cleaning event this year. We've been given an opportunity to divest ourselves of our excesses. We're left to discover what an amazing story can be told in the process. As the snow recedes into the woods, we see what is left behind. We look out at our tangible abundance. We see pieces of our history and our houses' histories that are no longer meaningful, helpful, or necessary, and we can let it all go.

Early on this cold, sunny Sunday morning, I drove over the roads in the town of Brighton, gently looking over piles of weathered accumulation townsfolk have gathered and placed by the roadside in anticipation of cleanup crews coming next week. Stories were shouting out to me. Pieces of our local history could be fashioned from some of these artifacts.

Nearly every person's pile of stuff offered old tires. Tires from cars we no longer own, or old, used tires, tread worn down to smoothness, sit by the road. These tires were once new. They carried drivers to the store, to school, to the hospital to have babies, to church on Sunday mornings, over miles of roads criss-crossing our hilly landscape.

I also noticed a surprising number of refrigerators parked out front. Some folks even had more than one. Many people had old stoves; some had old freezers, old washing machines, and old propane or kerosene stoves that used to heat old houses and camps nestled in our neighborhoods. All of these were big ticket items at one time. They started in some appliance store somewhere, and with great effort, were moved out here to our homes, decades ago.

Those stoves cooked family dinners, made tea and coffee, and baked bread. Those old freezers held a family's winter store of venison or beans from summer gardens. And those propane heaters kept families warm through winters that lasted for half a year or more, year after year. The refrigerators? They were once a family hub; they held milk, vegetables, and leftovers from Sunday chicken dinners, the tiny light inside a beacon of welcome for hungry family members.

Another category I noticed in the discard piles was bicycles, so many that I was amazed. All those spokes, tires, handlebars, chains, and gears. Years of riding on our beautiful back roads were represented. Some piles had little kid bikes of graduating sizes; others had big kid bikes with mashed tires or twisted frames. Behind some garages had been old bikes, tossed down after a last ride, or put aside for a repair job that never happened. Now they sit in a big pile of spring cleaning, not able to remember the riders with the wind on their faces, laughing in the sun.

In these big piles of castoffs are pieces of lives that used to be. Little kid rusty swing sets; old household fuel tanks, big enough for months of isolation; rusty gutters; old water pumps; old springs and beds that other people snuggled in; car parts, old tools, and broken chairs. In one pile I noticed an old tiller; it looked like a horse might have pulled it over the rocky dirt we walk on. The story it told was muted, but respectable. A patina of hard work was there under its rusty exterior.

Many piles in front of houses had old windows and doors in them. I was hypnotized by those artifacts. Windows that once were new, that once let pale winter light into our dark cabins and houses keeping out mosquitoes and flies, now sit in piles by the side of the road. Whose faces looked out of these portals to check on last night's snowfall, or to see if the rain had stopped? How many had been broken by a kid's unlucky baseball hit, or the shock of a tumbling white pine branch in the wind? So many windows, no longer needed, caught this early Sunday sun. We could look into the past through them, if we tried.

And the doors? What rooms did they close off? What privacies were gained, what warmth in the winter? How many were slammed in anger, or gently latched after checking on a sick child? They sit there, in these huge piles of spring cleaning, their jobs done, ready to free up space in someone's barn or basement, finished with the work of opening and closing pieces of lives which have moved on.

I was touched by discarded pieces of childhood: small Hot Wheels, old sandboxes, big rusty metal toy trucks, crooked doll houses. These toys all tell us of kids who are now older, who have moved on to other lives. Artifacts don't remember imaginative play of young ones, but somewhere, someone does.

Chicken wire, old stove pipe, TVs and typewriters, old engine blocks, snow blowers, antennas, end tables and broken lawn chairs— what we no longer need, want, or can use has appeared in roadside heaps around the town, to tell a story or two, before being carried away. Did we sit in the lawn chair, relaxing after a long day, or did we climb a high roof to put up that antenna? How deep was the snow the last time that blower worked?

Some people, driving by, find just the thing they were looking for, in someone else's pile. A true community of give and take is created. Harold needed a desk, but was tossing a file cabinet that Joe wanted; Marie was getting rid of her old lawn tractor, but found a working Crock-Pot. Niches are filled in the days before the cleanup crews arrive. Smiles are exchanged; neighbors join in conversation and recollection.

Epilogue: The swollen river is winter's excess being carried away to the ocean. Our piles of used-to-be will be carried away, too, in an eager release of spring cleaning. A letting go of memory makes room for the rest of our lives.

After earthquakes

I sat down in the Blue Moon Café in Saranac Lake after visiting a friend in the hospital on Sunday morning. She'd just had surgery, and when I arrived, was gingerly walking the hallway, well on her way to recovery. Her life was going to be very different now, with many difficult medical changes some of us go through at one time or another. Lovely bouquets of spring flowers were inside by her bed, bright yellow daffodils grew by the front door in the sun.

Outside the air was cool and the sun was brilliant. On Main Street, as I looked out the café window, sunlight was startling, shining off car windows driving by. After starting the day yesterday with the strange excitement of an earthquake, today began more thoughtfully, quieter, and with a full day's worth of gentle cogitation behind me.

Once by two, people entered the café looking around for available seats, finding a niche for themselves. Some immediately walked over to the coffee canisters and grabbed themselves a cup of joe before sitting down. I overheard folks chatting about their plans for the upcoming day: "I'm gonna do some outside chores today, what'r'you gonna do?" and "I'm going to Plattsburgh to get some garden supplies." And "I'm gonna wash my car." The list was interesting and productive, for most of us had the day off from our workaday lives.

Many people were touching base with one another for the first time since Saturday morning, after their own personal experiences with the earthquake. "Did it wake you up?" or "Did you feel any of the aftershocks?" or "Did you see the picture of the caved-in road on the Weather Channel?" or "Didja see us in the *New York Times*? Page 36 today, I think it was."

This minor earthquake happened to all of us, in one way or another. People from other parts of the country called friends and family in our area to hear our reports, to check on our safety. It made the national news, putting our neck of the woods on the map again, only this time we weren't the nation's cold spot, as is often the case when we hit the national airwaves. This time the earth moved under our feet, and rattled our homes and churches, in a big way.

We reassured one another; we compared notes about whether knick-knacks fell down, or if pictures were knocked off the walls, or if chimneys cracked. And we all remembered what a long time it felt like while the world was trembling and growling as our day began. Seconds felt like minutes, all the while leaving us unsure of how bad it really could get if it kept up.

An earthquake happens when internal pressures make pieces of the planet shift. It is sudden, it is startling, and it disrupts us from continuing activities as usual. An earthquake reminds us of how small we are compared with an entire planet. And that smallness gives a perspective we sometimes lose when we cling to routines in our ordinary days, and the tiny soap operas we all live through.

What happens when we struggle with personal internal pressures? Sometimes we endure quietly, and trust that time will make decisions for us. Other times we might snap. We could yell at the guy who cuts in front of us in traffic; we could hang up rudely on a bill collector on the phone; or we could answer someone's questions with a rude and sarcastic remark. Pressures within cause actions on the outside that might not be predictable, or even in line with our true personalities.

Sharing those pressures is one way to take the edge off. Talking with friends at a coffee shop is one way. Keeping a journal is another. Or, as my first post-quake instinct directed me, getting outside, and absorbing the stability of trees, ducks and rivers, is another.

My friend in the hospital was enduring her own internal quake, with a powerful dignity that showed a strong internal foundation of positivism, able to endure and persevere no matter the current pressures. Some things we just cannot control, like earthquakes, disease, and terrorist attacks on skyscrapers.

But there are some things we can control—our responses to these events. If we work at positivism, we can learn lessons every single day, no matter how abruptly our lives change. If we're sick, we learn how beautiful and precious a gift good health is, and we can strive to achieve it. If we endure an earthquake, with only a little temporary fear as a consequence, we might learn how lucky we are not to live somewhere where serious earthquakes are a commonplace occurrence. And if we unite as a country after a terrorist attack, we learn something about what is missing when complacency takes over.

When I'd walked into the Blue Moon, music was playing. Stevie Nicks was singing a new version of an old song, one that'd been very poignant to me in earlier years, called *Landslide*. The first words my ears picked up were: "Climb a mountain then turn around, and if you see your reflection in the snow-covered hills, well, the landslide will bring it down." It reminded me that everything changes except change itself, and that sometimes quite unexpectedly, lessons are there for the learning every day.

And from the same song: "Time makes you bolder, even children get older, and I'm getting older too." The stuff of wisdom, I'd say, washed down with good coffee, and the musical chatter of people gathered in a small town café, all of us rocked by forces of a planet responding to pressure, on a certain Saturday in April, when spring tried to settle in before its time.

Perimeter route

This morning I went for a walk around my town, a literal walk-about, as close to a perimeter route as I could muster. As I walked, I took notes on the people and small places in the community of Saranac Lake, a walking snapshot of the first Sunday morning in June.

Parking my car at Kinney's, I began my walk by heading out on Ampersand Avenue, past the tennis courts where a group of four women was playing doubles, on a windy, cool morning. They were having fun. Houses I passed were decorated with blooming lilac bushes, the heavenly sweet aromas smelling light purple to me.

A constant hum of lawnmowers filled the air, if not directly on the particular street I was on, then on the next street over. With so many freshly mowed lawns, the smell of cut grass permeated my senses deliciously. Many colorful window boxes sported fresh blooming flowers, and people were out planting annuals in their flower beds.

I noticed "hidden" trails, where local folks make short cuts between streets, down hills, behind houses, and through the woods. A few times, I took those paths, and saw why they were created: to get from "here" to "there" made sense with a shortcut, especially if viewed through the eyes of kids growing up in the neighborhood. A train whistle blew in the distance.

Keeping to the outside of the village, I stayed along the invisible line where forest meets civilization. Here we've carved a niche in the natural world for ourselves. We've built homes over the decades, poured sidewalks, and crawled up hills and alongside riverbanks to do it. And in many cases, we kept some majestic trees on the property, literally living in the woods, even within village limits.

Examples of old stone walls filled my eyes on some village streets. Some walls sit where a building used to be, others hold hillsides up, so they don't melt into roads, or sink after a house is built on top. Some walls were reinforced with cement, some were completely rebuilt with cement blocks, but some were original, round rocks lifted and piled together by some earlier hands, creating security for mountain civilization.

I learned about the flow of water, after some recent rainfalls gave us some to watch in motion. I could tell where streams might have

photo by Colin Surprenant

Broadway

been before we came to these hillsides to build our homes, flowing
from up high to down low, from Lake Colby to Lower Saranac, from
the hills down to the river: water goes where water needs to go, and
builders took that into consideration when they built streets and
houses in our town.

Many friendly people were out walking, friendly groups of two,
or busy singletons. We said, "Hi, how's it going?" and smiled as we
passed. We were all stretching our legs, climbing hilly roads, walking
alongside homes where Sunday breakfasts were being made. I smelled
bacon cooking a couple of times, and banana bread somewhere else.

On the Lake Street hillside, I looked into the woods, and saw a
carpet of pale blue forget-me-nots in profusion on the forest floor.
The sight of thousands of tiny blue flowers was soft and delicate to
the eye, looking like pieces of sky sprinkled on the ground.

When I looked out over Lake Flower, the view of McKenzie and
Haystack was as clear as I'd ever seen it, making those close-by mountains look both protective and powerful at the same time.

After walking through Riverside Park, I visited with nineteen
Canada geese, prowling around the shoreline near the boat launch. I
walked right into their flock, thinking they would take off, but they
seem very accustomed to human attention, and continued eating
grass, challenging one another for leadership, honking softly, and dip-

ping in the river, graceful as swans. Their long necks were regal, their black beaks and legs leathery and tough looking.

Reaching the railroad crossing on Pine Street just as I'd wished, a train was coming, blowing its horn, ringing its bells. I stood and watched its slow approach, the careful holding to the track, and heard the intense sound of heavy iron and steel grinding together, mere feet from my eyes. These were sounds from another era, and represented a brief flash of time travel. Long ago, people came to our neck of the woods on trains. The ride was so much more comfortable than stage-coaches on rutted dirt roads! Passengers waved as the train passed by, and I waved back. I reminded myself to plan another train trip one of these days. Train people understand the call of the rails.

Continuing my circle route, I passed wonderful, cared-for homes of many styles, in inviting and cozy neighborhoods. Nestled in hill-sides, by ponds and rivers, and behind big trees, our houses are fasci-nating to look at. Some are sophisticated, some strewn with the joyful sight of kids' toys. I saw one small house in its own cedar grove, nes-tled in, back from the road. So many hidden pieces of village life teased my imagination.

There was no doubt about the quality of life I observed this morning. Saranac Lake is a lovely community, with neighborhoods full of charismatic houses to live in, surrounded by the bounties of nature, and inhabited by true Adirondack souls. A peaceful feeling filled this Sunday morning, an invitation to sit back and read the paper over a cup of coffee, before mowing the lawn, putting up the railing, or planting those window boxes.

Try walking around your home town some day, literally. It's fun, and it's healthy. Connections and stories unfold in all the nooks and crannies you'll discover when you do.

Adirondack archeology

Archeology is the study of past human life as revealed by relics left by ancient peoples. Place that definition side by side with the fact that the short human history in these north woods is not old enough to be called ancient. Humans mostly mark history in terms of human activity. These mountains have not been settled since the 1600s or 1700s like some of the older ports on America's eastern coast, nor are there native artifacts from earlier Indian settlements, nor do we have ancient Roman or Greek stories to tell like some old spots in Europe. Most human habitation here has occurred in the past 150 years or so.

What a hearty bunch those early Adirondackers were! Horses pulled coaches and sleds over extremely intense terrain. We know what their winters were like, and we know how long it takes to walk miles to school. Some of us even know how cold our uninsulated cabins can get, and how it feels to chop firewood out of frozen woodpiles when a spring cold snap lasts a little too long.

But those early settlers stuck it out, and elbowed in a spot in these mountains to call home. They left their niche to us, watchers from a couple generations later.

Artifacts left by those early settlers are not ancient, but they're as old as old stuff can be found around here. Some true relics can be found while hiking in area forests. I take delight in these discovered treasures. Each one tells a story, or at least tries to.

I was with a group of friends one autumn, sitting around a campfire. I walked into the woods a ways following someone's dog which had taken off, dragging a leash behind it.

I caught the dog at the same time something unnatural-looking in the underbrush caught my eye. I grabbed it, twisting it free from the raspberry bushes it was under. I was no wiser for holding it in my hand.

A rusty metal cylinder with a narrow diameter was attached to a rusted gauge with wires dangling from it. Amazing treasure. None of my friends had a clue. It had a knob place, but no knob. We noticed a small metal connector piece at the bottom, where a nut and bolt would be appropriate. There was a story here. I looked around for something else under the brambles to give me a clue...no luck. Some

Mixing nature and old relics—an abandoned car in Brighton

time ago this thing was new. It was attached to something; it had a purpose. Now it was fodder for the imagination of a generation which probably had never seen whatever home appliance it once belonged to. We guessed it was from the fifties, maybe forties...or maybe outer space.

A lot of Adirondack archeology is like that. I have a few chunks of large rusty molded metal in my personal archeological collection. One large piece I pulled up from the river bed might have come from huge metal machinery in an old hydro dam upstream, now gone. Another piece looked like an old lightning rod from the small barn on our property; someone told us lightning actually killed a person right at the front door of the barn decades earlier. It might just be a plant holder, though.

Abandoned dumps are near every settlement in these parts. In the early days folks just dumped unwanted stuff in the woods, and went home. One abandoned dump near my house has an old car, and half of another one. You can tell small mammals find refuge in those sturdy frames. Scattered in the forest are many bottles and cans, barrels, oil cans, old stoves, big barn buckets and tins. In early spring, wildflowers grow up and over this dump, followed later in the spring by ferns whose delicate green lace makes the spot heavenly. Nature is so forgiving.

Some bottles and cans are pretty old and interesting. They sport names of local dairies, or stores that no longer exist, from towns that are right nearby. They charmingly tease the observer to think about ·

local history. Just think about the folks who carved out the spot we live in. Think of the day they made their "dump run" and dropped these treasures down the hillside, without a second thought, and just went home.

The woods were the same as they are now. Rivers flowed in the same direction they do now. The sun made shadows on forest floors where chipmunks scurried, and chickadees chirped. Those people moved about their days much the same as we do now, one season at a time, surviving.

So, although not ancient, the weather-beaten sturdy remains from our predecessors are clues to what touched their lives, what was on their shelves and in their barns, and what they had to take to the dump, in the days before we were born.

Today I attended the Brighton History Day at Asplin Tree Farm in Gabriels. The building was filled with displays of the old houses and families from earliest times in this township. Many of the first people were guides, and others worked at providing hospitality to visitors. We had trains and stagecoaches, and beautiful boats on the lakes. We had lots of houses and hotels that had burned, and other homes and camps that were rebuilt. We had poor folks and rich folks, and lovely churches.

Most interesting to me was getting a chance to see the faces of people whose artifacts I had been noticing over the years in the abandoned dumps in the woods. I reached out to touch a few who I knew lived on my road. I saw what their houses looked like, and what kinds of clothes they wore. I studied the serious souls looking back out of those old photographs, and I accepted the challenge to belong here just as they did. At 2 p.m., all those in attendance at the History Day gathered for a community photo.

I made sure my face could be seen smiling up at the photographer, with two of my sons standing in front of me. I was happy and proud to be there with some of the elders of the community, along with some of the youngest kids of the town. I wanted someone a hundred years from now to make contact with my face, my presence in the community in the woods in the year 2000, in a future Brighton History Day. The old dumps would probably still be there for exploring, but my bottles and cans won't.

They'll have to settle for the photograph, and me looking right back at them, offering them the same challenge offered me: to belong here, to these grand woods and lonely roads of the North Country.

Brighton History Day 2000

photo by Pat Willis

Running

For the third day in a row, in the middle of half a dozen commitments and responsibilities, I laced up my running shoes, grabbed my hiking poles, and took off for the woods. Why?

I needed to think. Time spent hiking, walking, biking, or running is therapeutic for those of us finding ourselves overextended and worried about fitting all the daily pieces together.

When I go out for a run, I start off slowly. I breathe in smells of cedar and balsam as I enter the forest. I hear the familiar chatter of chipmunks and red squirrels. I take note of the dry conditions, and try to remember the last soaking rain. I listen for the birds' songs, and overhead I hear the high whistle of a hawk. My poles dig in, and my legs push off, over and over as I climb the esker.

I start to lose my breath a little, then quickly, exercise mode kicks in, and I'm an athlete, with regular deep breathing, quick heartbeats, and sweat on the back of my neck.

Strong arms grip the poles, and my legs tell me when it's their time to let loose and run. Once running, I am the same soul I've always been as a runner: slow, earnest and rhythmic. Sometimes a hill will slow me down, sometimes not. But I persevere.

Once in my running-machine mode, my mind is free to sort through the brambles of a busy life.

One example is just this: There is just too much to do around these parts in the summer! We live in an isolated splendor, with gorgeous scenery, great wildlife, and very few people. In the summer, visitors come from every direction, from every conceivable spot on the planet, to join our wonderland.

Among these guests are some of the world's best athletes, who are, as I write, biking their hearts out on 112 miles of our beautiful roads in the Lake Placid Ironman triathlon race. In the area at the same time are some of the world's best trumpet players, attending the International Trumpet Seminar at the Lake Placid Institute. For the upcoming weekend, Lake Placid will host the Rebecca Kelly Dance world premiere of *Wilderness Suite*, with music by world-renowned composer Richard Adler.

The word "world" keeps cropping up. For all our quiet isolation, the world comes to us, especially in the summertime. Those of us whose imaginations are stimulated by possibilities of life's offerings are drawn to these gifts.

We have theatrical performances in Westport, at the Depot Theatre. Right here in Saranac Lake, Pendragon Theatre is offering three plays in repertory, with amazing skill and variety, week after week.

The Lake Placid Center for the Arts has a summer schedule full of exciting options. Wonderful lectures are being put on by Adirondack Discovery and the Adirondack Museum in Blue Mountain Lake. Long Lake has a lively arts community. In Jay, there is JEMS, Jay Entertainment and Music Society. Great workshops are offered by the Adirondack Park Visitor Interpretive Centers in Newcomb and Paul Smiths. Loon Lake offers us Loon Lake Live! with top notch classical music concerts and talks, and there are interesting presentations being offered by the nascent Natural History Museum of the Adirondacks in Tupper Lake.

There's more, too, but just listing this cornucopia of possible activity boggles my mind. I'm out running in the woods, trying to prioritize, counting hours in the days, days in the week, figuring out how to create another great summer in the Adirondacks, and see everything being offered.

On top of all those fledgling ideas, comes a wave of background chatter. I'm running a busy household with summer visitors, getting up at 5 a.m. every day of the week, trying to assemble a family unit for occasional meals, taking kids out to practice driving, trying to find a way to get the mice to move back outdoors, and trying to make appointments to get the oil changed for three cars used by four drivers working in three towns.

Back to running.

Running is a constant, no matter how long the lists of "things to do" are. The familiar strength of moving muscles, the welcome sweat rolling down my face—these are constants, season after season, year after year. It's a component of who I am.

Making room in a busy day for a run is a spiritual gift. It temporarily removes you from your pile of bills or sink of dirty dishes. The phone disappears. You give yourself a moment in nature, with air and sky and the high whistle of hawks.

Something gets through to you, some beacon of correctness, some message from the planet itself. And when you're done, you've been fortified. Reassured that you know something important, something usually unsaid, you can tackle your lists and obligations with some inner wisdom and confidence. Those endorphins are great.

After all, it is any athlete's reward. And when and where better to reap that reward than during the glorious summers in the Adirondacks.

After washing windows

Friday was deliciously warm, especially for the end of October. Having watched the weather forecast, I knew "real" weather was heading our way, so these breezy 60s felt like mid-summer to me. I dashed outside to take laundry off the line with shorts on, in my bare feet. Damp leaves stuck to the bottoms of my feet with an eerie feeling—perhaps I had never done this autumn barefooting before. I felt like a kid, enjoying a gift.

My husband Neil was washing windows, and after each one was done, brightness inside was immediate. Looking out was more like letting the outdoors in. Plenty of light and space was out there now that the leaves were all down. We puttered around the house until we got hungry, and day had dimmed to dusk. Since the kids were out and about in their own whirlwinds of activity, we decided to go out to eat. Dependably, a handful of dining options exists in our neck of the woods, so we settled on one of our favorites, the Belvedere. One reason we made that choice was that we had a lot to talk about, and the Bel offers both atmosphere and time to talk.

While Neil went in to see if a table would be available in less than 45 minutes, I stood out back in their parking lot. A warm breeze tumbled stray leaves about in the dark. I gazed up at lights on the side of Helen Hill, clearly visible over the train tracks. Here was a beautiful view: the poetry of a cozy village, hills dotted with homes, windows lit from within, smiling out at me, just standing in a parking lot at the end of a busy week. It nearly brought a tear to my eye. I appreciate this lovely little town, and the continuous act of discovering why I do brings me joy.

We only had a twenty-minute wait, so we sat in the bar. People came and went, laughing. A woman walked in with a funny little dog, which seemed to know right where to sit. The bar maid dropped and broke a glass, and everyone gave her a good-natured hard time, and she laughed, too.

Sometimes we shoot a game of pool while we wait, but today we had a chance to visit with some friends for a little bit; they were waiting for their table, too. We talked about all our sons, based on years of intertwined child raising. Some years we were sitting side by side at basketball games, or soccer games, or supervising overnights at one home or the other. We talked about our impending empty nests, some local news, and then our respective tables were called, and we were seated in the dining room.

While in the process of reading over the familiar menu, we noticed another couple sitting nearby who also had sons whose lives were intertwined with our boys', and we chatted a few minutes with them about the senior play, which was in less than a week, and upcoming soccer playoffs, where our boys were playing for the league championship.

I was taken by the sense of community we all partake in. These offspring of the other diners were sprinkled throughout our family photo albums over the years; the once little boys were now young men. In that one moment, we were three couples dining at a friendly family restaurant. We had raised seven boys in our community, full of good times, lessons learned, pride, discovery, and hard work. And amazingly, it was all during the same twenty-or-so years wedge of time.

And on a warm autumn night, we all were listening to the same quiet chatter and laughter, the same glasses clinking together as tables were cleared, the same yummy warm bread being brought by while we waited for our meals.

Other patrons shared their Friday evenings with one another, too. I noticed them stopping by to visit with other guests as they'd leave, or saying to the waitress, "See you next week!" as they left the tip on the table.

Other towns have places like this, I know. I gravitate towards them when I travel. They tell a story about the town, and bring some glue to hectic lives everyone seems to be leading these days. The Belvedere is a piece of our Adirondack life, where people come together, eat, laugh, and talk, and then move on to their other responsibilities. It creates an oasis, as well as a full belly. The great view of the backside of Helen Hill at night is a surprisingly sweet addition while parking the car.

Years of gathering have occurred here, and years more will. This is not a fancy, get-all-dressed-up dining experience; it is a belonging-to-your-community, catching-up-after-a-busy-day, blue jeans kind of place. And it feels just right, as we begin to hunker down for winter, all of us, here in our neck of the woods.

Today I'll just pull out my little container of leftover lasagna, and warm it up. I'll watch snow sprinkle down outside, through clean shiny windows, and be glad for it all. We find our luck in surprising places, and one is having a great gathering place to talk among friends while autumn shifts into what comes next.

Small miracles

Today started out an ordinary day. Up at 5 a.m., fix a cup of tea, and throw an extra log on the fire in the woodstove. Quiet.

Driving to work toward Saranac Lake, a long line of cars developed behind a school bus, which was stopping every so often along the route to pick up students. Usually this stop and go was frustrating; people who want to get to work on time send out negative vibes as they wait impatiently to make their way in this slow train. But a small miracle occurred. The school bus pulled over, and we all drove past, at our own comfortable pace. I want to thank wholeheartedly every school bus driver who pulls over to let a line of waiting cars go by. You may not know that that one simple act reduces stress in so many people, but it does, and we thank you.

Passing through Gabriels, I nearly drove off the road as I watched the sun rise. Our friendly local star was a huge deep orange globe, much bigger than I imagine when I think of the sun. It was almost frightening. Peeking over the side of Esther Mountain, it slowly rose, in its orange roundness, to become our beacon for the day. All around the open fields, long silky clouds of fog and mist swirled. Poking over the top of these low clouds were pointed tops of the tallest pine trees, poking upward in their triangular way, distinctive and powerfully Adirondack. Around the rising sun, higher clouds were pale pink and welcoming. That big orange ball was a planetary miracle, and I was awed, humbled and appreciative as I continued into town.

Once in Saranac Lake, the coffee at Hyde's was delicious, and fresh-out-of-the-oven muffins from the Blue Moon Café were still warm, and full of sweet, tart berries. I was counting my blessings as I arrived at Petrova Middle School and found my spot for the day, being a substitute math teacher.

At lunch time, we held a meeting for middle school students on the Saranac Lake *Echo* school newspaper staff. The room was full of earnest kids, all with ideas for what to put into the next paper, what deadlines they could make, who would take pictures, and who would help with the computer. I was in the presence of a wondrous experience of young people giving their time and effort for creating a school paper that would tell the world something about their lives as students. Considering today was report card day, and the day they received their school pictures, and the weather outside was absolutely wonderful, I was proud and impressed that these people stayed indoors during lunchtime to work on this meaningful school-journalism project. A minor miracle, in itself.

After school, driving to Lake Placid, I pulled around the last corner, and reduced my speed. I was stunned silent at the sudden huge beauty of Whiteface Mountain at that precise and unique moment. The mountaintop was pure white and edgy, pointed and sharp like a volcano. The sun shone on it so brightly, the lower portion of the mountain was golden, almost luminescent. I shook my head realizing it was the same amazing sun that I'd admired just this morning.

I felt I was on another planet; on this magical day, the majestic mountain was ironically placed right near where I needed to be. I pulled into a parking lot, and stood there, just staring. Here was beauty and wonder popping into my day again, and me getting my socks knocked off once more. What a miracle.

I got home with just enough time to change my clothes, grab my hiking poles, and get to the trails at the Visitor Interpretive Center. My last hike had been slippery and cold, after several snowfalls, and I thought I wouldn't see the earthy colors again until spring. But here they were, just at dusk, and the smells were rich and musty. I stayed near the water, hoping to catch a glimpse of a sunset, and instead, I caught a glimpse of a swift golden pre-sunset moment.

The same big orange globe I'd seen coming up this morning, and glowing on Whiteface Mountain this afternoon, was here now, caught between two layers of clouds on its way back down to the horizon. Clouds were peachy colored, and the sun's rays filtered between them briefly, turning the water to a shimmery silver, like mercury. By the time I'd circled the marsh, the moon was rising, becoming brighter and higher as I walked.

Looking into the water as I crossed the bridge, I saw the white, olive-shaped reflection shining back at me, looking like a winking friend. The last time I'd been there, that water had been covered with ice. Just this one extra day of sweet liquid lapping sounds of pond on bridge, and moonlight sparkling in water, was a miracle to me.

I called it a day of small miracles because of the humble appreciation for where I was in time and space today. A series of unpleasant situations had been scattered throughout the day as well, as many of us must endure in any given ordinary day. I'd been allowing those unpleasantries to get me down. But somehow, the spirit of the Adirondacks pulled me out of the funk, and the spirit of the planet put everything into perspective.

Small miracles are everywhere. Maybe you, too, can find a cure for what's bothering you in a stunning sunrise, or a quiet walk in the woods when the moon's reflection smiles at you. You'll never know unless you give it a try.

Season's end

Just last week the season's lovely blue gentians were in bloom alongside a well-used trail at the Adirondack Park Visitor Interpretive Center. Their pretty blue cup-like flowers are sturdy and striking at the end of summer. That bright color blue catches your eye when you walk by. Seeing those flowers always takes me back to another time in Saranac Lake, when the scenery in town was different, and those lovely blue blossoms were painted on walls of a little restaurant called the Blue Gentian.

Located on Main Street, the Blue Gentian occupied the building which is now home to Corvo's restaurant. Distinctively decorated in those days, it looked like a Bavarian café. The Blue Gentian was one of the busiest seasonal eateries in town. Waitresses wore full skirts patterned with flowers, white shirts and aprons. They were monitored by the business owner, a no-nonsense old world European woman named Meta J. Bofinger, known to many as Miss Bo.

Miss Bo was a short, square-shaped, hard-working woman who took enormous pride in her restaurant. She spoke with a strong German accent, and her light eyes twinkled when she was happy.

Regular customers returned summer after summer, and tourists delighted in their "discovery" of a little bit of Europe in the heart of the Adirondacks. Many of these folks wanted to compliment the chef for her delicious entrees, scrumptious desserts, and her world-famous sour cream raisin pie, piled high with golden meringue. Miss Bo would happily come out front to chat with a fan, her face beaded with sweat from the kitchen, but smiling nonetheless.

The Blue Gentian opened in the 1930s, I'm told, and was one of the town's "institutions" for more than forty years. I'm not entirely certain when it closed its doors for the last time, but for many years after, I'd see Miss Bo in town, and I'd stop to chat with her.

I'd been one of her waitresses back in the 1970s, and always respected her business savvy and her skill in the kitchen. She demonstrated what a good work ethic looked like. For me learning that subject, there was no better teacher.

A number of "institutions" from back in the old days in Saranac Lake are now mere memories. Remember Wilson's department store, the Berkeley Hotel, the Army-Navy store, Altman's "four doors to four floors of fine feminine fashion," Newberry's, Alice's Restaurant, the Berkeley Theater, and the Oxford Market?

These places were destination businesses. You would enter their doors because you needed something, something to wear, or something to eat, or a chance to watch a movie, or have a quick cup of coffee with breakfast. The town in those days was different than it is now. More small stores welcomed local shoppers, and shopkeepers and workers would often know your name. A more noticeable semblance of the town stretched to take care of the needs of people in the community.

Soon now Ames department store will be closing its doors for the last time. Although it is on the outskirts of town, it, too, has long been a town "institution." Ames is the place people would go for curtain rods, motor oil, work shirts, socks, alarm clocks, Halloween costumes or school supplies. It helped us survive a broken clothesline, or supply a last-minute birthday card, or find a new pair of jeans for a fast-growing nine-year-old whose ankles were suddenly showing.

But Ames was not beautiful or quaint. It was just full of the stuff of our lives. Once Newberry's closed, Ames was the most versatile stop on a local shopping day. It functioned to serve members of the community, and its season is almost over.

There are places where we spend our money that we've incorporated into our ordinary days. They are part of our living-here network. We move by their windows and doors, entering, shopping, and leaving, creating a footprint of what is needed, offered and appreciated in our town at any given time.

We're looking at a different era soon, one without the many conveniences supplied by Ames. Maybe now our town will hatch another kind of season, with new stores coming in like the old Wilson's or Altman's to provide us with our clothes, and friendly salespeople who welcome us through their doors. Maybe there will be a dining spot offering a slice of pie and cup of coffee, or better yet, a movie theater popping popcorn at 6 p.m. every night, welcoming us into our hometown.

One can only hope.

Morning swim

I am a lucky person. I enjoy swimming, and I live near a beautiful swimming pool. During the college fall and spring semesters, "my" pool is staffed by trained lifeguards. The water is usually warm enough to be inviting. The inside air temperature is always warm and humid, like some summer days.

I get up early, have a cup of tea, then pack my gym bag. Fresh towels, clean clothes, shampoo. As soon as *SportsCenter* is over, I warm up the car, wake up my son, and I'm off.

When I get to the pool, my heart always races. Will the lifeguard show up? After all, guards here are teenagers, most of them, and 6 a.m. is not an hour when most people that age shine. I forgive them their lapses, but feel horrible when my swim is cancelled.

But once the lifeguard arrives, and the door is unlocked, I am free to swim. I stand at the deep end, on the edge of the pool, and I stretch my long muscles. I bend and dive into a liquid mirror.

Water is kind, with dependable buoyancy, both quenching and gentle. Back to primordial ooze, or embryonic fluid, there is always a sense of return.

I am usually the first person in the water. And when I dive in, I make the first small waves on the silvery surface. I do the breast-stroke, so I don't make a lot of waves, but once the waves begin, they multiply like crazy. I always think about this as I watch the first wave hit the side of the pool, careen off the edge, and become two, followed quickly by two more. Pretty soon, it's wavy water throughout the entire pool.

I think about waves I make in my dry-land life, too. Everything we do ripples its effects throughout our days and lives. A word spoken here, a deed performed there, all these turn into pivots for other people, and then others still are changed by those.

By the time I get to the other side of the pool, I am swimming in almost turbulent water. Waves are present in this pool due to my actions, my arms pulling water through water, my legs kicking. All me, all this aquatic activity because of me.

I remember being a kid, and the rush of happiness I'd get when I knew I could go swimming. How everyone I knew had that same rush—summer, water, waves, and splashing. So daily, when I dive into this pool, the little kid in me just grins.

I've learned a lot in my twenty plus years of being a morning swimmer. For example, I've learned that goggles are very important. Keeping your eyes securely away from chemically treated water helps the rest of your day go better: no squinting, rubbing red eyes, or crying. It just makes sense to protect them. And goggles are small; the sport of swimming does not carry much baggage.

Bathing suits only last so long, with constant contact with chlorinated water, so you should always have a spare. I've found most suits degrade rapidly once the first sign of material unraveling happens, and daily swimming keeps my suits' lifespans at around six months or less.

I've learned it takes a certain kind of person to be a morning swimmer. You must be someone who likes to swim, and likes to get up in the morning, and lives somewhere near a pool or body of water.

These folks like quiet, which is what a morning swim is. They build muscles with repetition after repetition of the same long body motions. Some of us count laps, back and forth, using a variety of methods. There are 36 laps to a mile in my pool. You've got to be able to count. It's often hypnotic, the counting without thinking of anything else. Rhythm. Peace. Zen.

Different swimmers prefer different strokes, and circuits of many strokes. You can stretch and reach and pull and kick in a wide variety of combinations, many learned when we were kids taking swimming lessons.

One of the nicest components of an early morning swim is that it is not rough. There is no jarring, like with road-running, or treadmill running, or basketball playing. You can swim even when you have a sore knee, hip or ankle. You just swim gently.

It is warm at the pool, and a controlled environment, which is dependable, predictable and pleasant. It is liberating in its dependability, unlike with running when you are a slave to the fickleness of weather outdoors. It feels like summer in the pool, even when it is twenty below zero outside.

You can meditate while you swim. Counting repetitively, lap after lap, stroke after stroke, your mind can reach a peaceful, non-worried state.

You can also think about your future, or challenges on the job, or

Liquid mirror—Paul Smith's College swimming pool

figure out which car needs the next oil change. Little brain tweaks you might have had gnawing at you can disentangle while you add laps to your count.

You can set daily athletic goals for yourself (more laps, faster times, different strokes added), or not. No one will know but you. But at the end, when you pull yourself out of the pool, you've been alive. You've moved your body through space and time without walking, using long muscles and breathing warm air. You've worked, and been rewarded with endorphins, and the rest of your day will unfold better because of it.

In my neck of the woods there are a few places where a person can swim during winter months. I know there are some schools and hotels in our hundred-mile radius that also have pools open to the public at certain times. Swimming is a fun activity, able to be enjoyed by all generations. Give it a moment's thought: it might offer you a possibility for staying in shape, or venturing into a winter fitness program.

By the way, pools are open at all times of the day. Lunch time swims and evening swims might be easier for some than my choice of 6 a.m. Any time would be good to give it a try. Swimming makes you strong. See if you don't agree.

photo by Colin Surprenant

100

Chapter 3

Mountain Culture:
What We All Understand

These mountain roads

Take a moment to think about the roads in your life, from macadam roads you drive on daily, to life's roads that brought you to this moment in time.

Roads weave through the mountains we live in, openings in the woods where someone has gone before. Some roads make perfect sense; they wind alongside rivers which themselves have blazed paths through the uneven terrain for thousands of years. We see sensibility in following Mother Nature's lead; rivers flow downhill, generally towards other rivers, or big lakes, or even the ocean itself. They have purpose and direction.

Rivers were the earliest roads, long before the footpaths that followed along their banks. Rafts and canoes allowed early humans to get from one spot to the next, albeit with the difficulties of rapids, waterfalls, beaver dams and blowdown to overcome in the process. But in the old days, a person could get from one place to another without the need for much tree cutting or mountain climbing.

Early settlers used their feet for travel, and the cost to them was physical energy and time. It took hours to reach places that now take minutes to get to. But connections to other people are always important, so they made their way, regardless of how long it took.

Current mountain residents forget the labors of those who came before us. It was not an easy task to move to the mountains, to set up a life in higher elevations. Once a few folks settled, however, more followed, eventually using horses and wagons to bring families and supplies to the natural sanctuary they found. Once horses and carriages began making their way uphill, rough roads were improved to accommodate them.

Reasons to move to these challenging isolated locations existed. Some people came to work in lumber camps or sawmills. Some wanted to escape from a crowded, dirty city life. Land was cheap. Some folks cast their fates to the wind, and came to the mountains to start over. A few people were hosts to and guides for lowland visitors. There were fish to be caught, fur-bearing animals to be trapped, game to be hunted—in other words, a life could be imagined. A certain spirit would be drawn to this wilderness life, and it was.

Roads were built to reach these quiet places, often located on the banks of a river or pond. Some followed old foot paths, some followed deer trails, but in all cases, roads were built by people, for people, in order to create community. Early roads were not easy on horse-drawn wagons, but it was a beginning. Not just anyone had the gumption to climb these hills to create a niche in a world near nature and away from cities. But our predecessors did just that.

Today's roads through mountain country run the gamut from well-maintained interstates all the way down to abandoned logging or mining roads, barely discernable to the modern eye. They take us deep into the woods, around lakes, and over mountain passes. We do not often think about how these roads have helped us live here, but we should. We can almost always make our way downhill towards civilization on them, if necessary. Then we make our way back uphill to our wilderness homes when the time is right. Making your way is what a road is all about, after all.

So if you ever find an abandoned road winding through a forest, up a mountain, or along a stream, give thought to the work of those who came before us. They cut down trees by hand, and leveled the earth, making a way for those who might follow.

Our civilized history is a good deal shorter than the history of those who live downhill from us, but some time ago, good hard sweat and muscle were used to open up the possibility for a future for generations that would follow. That future is right here, right now, in the sweet air of a mountain life, enjoyed by strong, unique individuals. Roads, carved out of a daunting, rugged wilderness, made it all possible. Really, it's how each and every one of us got here, to this very moment in time.

Weaving

Don't take the uniqueness of our lives in these woods for granted. Even if you are not an exercise nut, a variety of surprise and reward can be found in some of our mountain springtime activities. Action doesn't have to be sweaty, or require a whole day of planned effort. It doesn't even have to be much different from your ordinary life here. It requires a special attention, that's all.

Belonging in the Adirondacks, or any mountain community, is enhanced and improved by moving your body through the environment you live in. There are dozens of ways to do this, and with the true arrival of our short spring season, fresh reminders of activity options are shoots poking their heads up out of the ground, fresh, eager and ready for you to try.

First, the most widely used manner of moving an Adirondack body throughout these forests and villages is by walking. Perambulation. I believe the steps we take weave us into the spirit of a place: Pounding feet of tired runners reaching the top of the Whiteface road race, tentative steps on the uneven hilly terrain of the French Hill neighborhood, unthinking steps from the car to the entrance of the grocery store, marching in Winter Carnival parades, or just walking a child in a stroller through town. All of these actions are placing us exactly right here in the now of our lives.

We breathe as we walk, taking in the fresh air we are blessed with. We can stroll with family members after a big meal; we can walk around Moody Pond catching up with an old friend, or just take a walk around the house after recent surgery, slowly working to regain our strength.

Some people walk dogs, happy to have an excuse to get outside and move around. Following the leash, they watch their animal actively engage with his environment, a nose going nuts with the world's inviting odors. A dog's job is to discover through smell what other mutt or animal has made his mark on that very spot in the universe. We watch, amazed.

If you have a friend who lives just a few blocks away, the walk to her door can remind you how lucky you are for the relationship, and proximity, as well as knowing that the act of walking there is good for you. Walking through town regularly, we feel the evolution of place, storefronts changing displays, new businesses opening and closing, and the reward of enjoying the village flowers lovingly planted in the VIS (Village Improvement Society) parks. We are weaving ourselves with our feet and our hearts into this place.

Another way to move through this earthly wilderness environment is by paddling. As soon as the ice is gone, those of us who can want to put canoes and kayaks in open water, and move from one place to another, low, close to the water's surface like the ducks, loons, and beavers we encounter. The water's surface is broken by the bow of the boat, and by the quiet tug of the paddle. You see swirls of water moved, and the wake of parted water as it ripples to shore. You feel the coolness of water environment, and hear sounds of nature normally hidden from humanity. When you look up, you see the shore sliding away, and you are somewhere else, engaging with the aquatic network we are so lucky to have close by.

Still another way to move through Adirondack spaces is on a bicycle. Acknowledging the many levels of ability, ambition and experience in cycling around these mountains, there is still something held in common by all riders. Once on your bike, you can begin to fly low over the land, with passing trees and driveways melting away as you pedal, wind on your face. Vistas of mountains and rivers and lakes open up around bends in the road. Hills challenge your muscles up and reward your efforts down, like geographic life lessons. Every mile you pass through belongs to you on that exact day. You have been there, with your eyes open wide, wind on your face, and your heart pumping.

Local runners all know about weaving themselves into the terrain. We all have our routes and routines, and familiar trees, brooks, and outcroppings as personal markers. Sometimes our running shoes have a relationship with these roads and trails and we support and fuel it with our running. I know I hear my own personal footbeats echoing with the hills, thanking me for the attention. We runners know how far we want to go, whose dogs might be out to chase us, whether the river is running high, and if the bugs are bad. We know when passing cars might be annoying, or when a landmark tree is being hammered by a pileated woodpecker. These observations help braid the physical moments of running with the natural world we run through. They are our gifts of belonging.

I strongly recommend giving conscious thought to this engagement with place the next time the opportunity comes to you. Maybe elect to walk with a friend at lunch break, or park your car at one end of town for your errands, taking time to notice the pieces of your world as you move through it. Make a weekend date with your kid to go for a bike ride, or plan a full moon hike up a mountain one night. When you go out to get the mail, go a little farther, just to listen to the birds.

This spring, decide to do one small thing differently, with attention. A deep satisfaction comes with these steps and heartbeats. Like making baskets out of individual reeds, weaving yourself into the life offered here by active experiences makes you strong, and much more able to carry life's load. Just ask those of us who already do!

Biting flies

Like with any true mountain living, outdoor activity in the Adirondacks is challenging when it comes to the ever-present, warm-weather battle of the flies. When I first came here I wished someone would put it all down on a piece of paper so I could study and learn. Now with years under my belt, let me tell you what I've pieced together, and we'll look at first flies first.

Blackflies

The first flies to come after snowmelt are blackflies, pesky little black critters circling around your face when you go outdoors in May. Their sheer numbers are overwhelming—a person can actually visualize the concept of millions of flies, for weeks on end. These bugs congregate intensely around moving water, like the streams and rivers we fish in and canoe upon.

Blackflies swarm around humans. They want to go near your facial openings—your eyes, nose, mouth and ears. They have no sense of invasion of personal space. Finding places where your clothes open to allow appendages out, they hover around a wrist, ankle or neck. But these small flies will not be able to land on you if you run fast enough, or enjoy bike riding as your outdoor exercise. So think fast and act fast, and you'll be safer.

What does a blackfly bite feel like? I'll tell you what it feels like to me: astounding. Sharp pinprick, and rapid swelling under tight skin. Hot and hard and sore, as though I'd been hit by a rock the day before, leaving a red bump that lasts at least a whole day. That is just one bite. On a bad day, receiving only one bite would be a blessing. So if you are going to live here or visit during this time of year (Locals think it is very funny to have visitors at this time of year!), what in heaven's name are you supposed to do?

Skin So Soft, by Avon, affectionately referred to as SSS, is one answer. A particular chemical formula exists in this beauty product which although a little greasy, has an endurable aroma. Wiping it on your exposed body parts does allow you to spend some time in mountain spring air sans blackflies. Personally, I mix SSS with Skintastic, just to be on the safe side. For your spring outdoor survival information, blackflies sleep at night.

Mosquitoes

Which biting critters come next, in the ever-expanding sequence of emerging life in the spring? Mosquitoes. Their season is much longer, running pretty much from May until August. They need us, and all warm-blooded animals with accessible skin. The best thing about their arrival is that some of us sigh, relieved that blackflies will be gone within a few days. These two fly seasons only overlap for a little while, when some locals take trips to more urban, fly-less areas for relief.

For those who don't know or remember what a mosquito bite feels like: You feel violated to have blood drawn by an insect, and a little nervous. You have learned that you could get sick from certain types of mosquito bites. The bites themselves make you itch, and big welts form on the skin when you do. You can be chewed by many mosquitoes at the same time, and it feels like torture if you are not protected. Mosquitoes never sleep. They like to discover victims at night, and if you're unlucky, you can wake up with an eyelid swollen shut by a bite. Others may have been kept up all night by the buzzing noise around their heads, reminding us of the amazing value of window screens without holes.

Somehow, running will keep them from landing on you, but won't make them leave once they have landed and begun to suck. Swimming is good sport for avoiding these bugs, but mosquitoes will find you during the moments entering and leaving the water. Bike riding keeps you away from them. Canoeing on lakes and ponds is a possible outdoor activity during mosquito season. River paddling sometimes takes you deep into mosquito country, so take bug dope with you when you go.

When mosquitoes are here, being outdoors is bearable if you use some insect repellent with DEET as an ingredient. Although DEET products repel these bugs and others, the chemicals are not healthy for skin, or for young children. Be extra careful to wash up once you are indoors for the day. Mosquitoes will go away, usually, after the nights get cold, sometime in late August or early September.

Deerflies

If it is a warm spring, deerflies will come to your attention during the day time by mid June. If you park somewhere in the woods, they circle your car and attack your windows. When you get out, they dive bomb your head. They circle around and around your person, making small flying airplane noises. They have landing on the top of your head (or other, highest spot of anatomy) as their goal. Deerflies are relatively big, and they are powerful. Their bite is a searing sting that feels downright rude. It leaves a welt with a bright red dot in the middle. They will even bite you through your T-shirts if necessary.

Deerflies are known to travel in groups, and a very annoying time can be had when you are outnumbered. If you find yourself surrounded by several deerflies, move! Run! Make it hard for them to land. You should be able to find relief within a quarter mile. The only problem is, when these flies are most abundant, in summer's finest hot weather, you can outrun one group only to find another waiting around the next bend.

If you wear a hat, you are mightily protected. These are not smart flies. They are confused when they try to land on your head and they find a hat there. That buys you time, and you can get away. Even better than wearing a hat is wearing a hat sprayed with bug dope. These flies are somewhat repelled by bug dope with DEET as a component. They also do not like the earthy citronella-based bug dopes (but neither do people). Deerflies can't catch you on a bike, and won't bother you much if you're out on a lake in a canoe.

If there is only one deerfly buzzing around you, you could hold very still until it lands on you, then swat it with your hitting hand. You can probably catch 80 percent of single deerflies if you hit them quickly before they bite you. Dragonflies love to eat deerflies, so if you have a personal deerfly problem and know where dragonflies hang out, move in that direction. You'll be impressed with the help these lacy wonder-bugs offer in major bug battles, snagging deerflies with panache.

Deerflies do not bother us at night or when it rains. And when nights get cold in late summer, they go away until the following year.

No-see-ums

As warm weather evolves, no-see-ums come. These invisible flies come during a warm night, as though from the air itself, finding you around a campfire, or talking to a neighbor in the driveway, or in your bedroom, entering through the tiny holes in your screens. They find you with their tiny sharp invisible mouths, and they are merciless. To fight these devils, you cannot invite them in. You must not leave lights on at night in rooms with opened screened windows. You will be defenseless if you do, and you won't want to stay. Some people I know spray their screens at night with any kind of bug dope spray they have on hand, and they say that tactic works.

Although the bites of no-see-ums are hugely surprising pinpricks and are startling, and quickly itchy, they generally do not leave horrible welts or next day reminders, as do the other flies I've mentioned. So a mild bug dope coating on exposed skin before bed, if you feel the room has filled up with tiny flies, could buy you enough time to fall asleep. They are warm weather nuisances, and we count their season as short.

Overview

Remember to minimize the use of perfumes, aromatic deodorants, shampoos and soaps during bug season. All the biting flies like sweet smells and seek out users of these odorous materials. Some people I know refuse to use powerful insect-fighting chemicals to repel bugs. Some take extra B vitamins or eat quantities of garlic to repel them from the inside out. Some take very infrequent showers. Some folks stay so busy and active that no biting bug will ever land on or bite them (so they say). And some folks spend a lot more time indoors in the summer than they'd like to, because the battle is fierce. However, you may be among those who find almost no interference with outdoor summer activities, especially if you live in a village.

The primary bugs I've found that bite without provocation in our neck of the woods are: blackflies, mosquitoes, deerflies and no-see-ums. There are others, of course, and in different areas, their seasons may be a little different. But here are ours, gathered on a list, to help you prepare for your active Adirondack outdoor experiences with less frustration, and more ammunition.

Wisdom like this is valuable, and the mountain summer is more beautiful when you can go out to play in the wild.

Father's Day

Father's Day was overcast and cool, the best kind of weather for me to generate thoughts. So this is what I thought today: If moms can be represented by Mother Earth, dads can be represented by Father Time. If you ask most teenagers, they will tell you moms have a tendency to linger over their mothering duties a little too long, while dads appreciate getting their own time back when the kids are big enough and have learned enough to move on. Dads don't usually have as much time as they'd like for many things.

For the most part, dads don't live as long as moms. Social science research projects and medical research labs have theorized why this happens for years. It doesn't change the fact that most of us will learn to say good-bye to our grandfathers before our grandmothers, and our dads before our moms.

So let's look at what we can do to give ourselves some gifts of appreciating our fathers. If your grandfather or father is alive, and you are able to be in his life, be in his life. Ask him questions. Tell him he is important to you. Learn from him.

If he is not around anymore, take time to think about contributions he made to your life, and be grateful for them.

When my dad passed away last year, I felt momentarily lost without his love and support. At the same time, I felt that he was somehow closer to me in spirit. I looked into my forest for some way to acknowledge that gift of closeness.

On one of my running trails, I adopted a tree. This tree is a huge white pine, between the trail (which represents my path in life) and the pond (which represents all the nourishment I've been given). This dad-tree is sturdy and tall, like I remember my dad from my childhood. It is too large to encircle with my arms, just as he was most of my life, until his final illness thinned him down to pole size. And this tree has mighty branches which spread wide, high above me, offering protection from the elements, and a roost for birds of the forest. When I first discovered it, shortly after Dad died, the tree was immediately familiar to me, as though it had a face I had always known.

I try to visit my dad-tree at least once a week, on a run or a trek, usually early in the morning. If I've needed some wisdom or support,

Hidden view in forest, Black Pond outlet, Paul Smiths

I lean on this tree, and try to remember what my dad would have said or suggested. What I always end up finding is a recollection of unconditional love, and the enormity of the gifts of wisdom he always gave. Although not brilliant, my dad was wise in many ways, and his deep voice was kind, imparting advice every chance he could, since he believed it was his job as a parent.

My own children appreciate their dad, and they know, as they find their way in this world, that his rational thought and knowledge are gifts he wants them to carry with them. Father's Day is a good day to think for a moment about what kinds of contributions your father, grandfather, stepfather, foster father or father figure has made to your life. What wisdom is in you now because they offered it?

- Do you carry a Swiss army knife?
- Do you like the Yankees or the Knicks or the Fighting Irish?
- Can you tie a necktie?
- Can you put a worm on a hook and catch a fish?
- Can you change the oil in your car?
- Do you climb mountains, or cross-country ski?
- Do you use his tips to balance your check book?
- Do you bake bread, or go hunting in the fall?

photo by Randy Lewis

Sparkling water

- Can you saw a two-by-four, hammer a nail, or paint a room?
- Can you toss a frisbee or program your VCR?
- Do you know stories from WWII or Vietnam?
- Do you know how rough old hands get gnarled and worn?

(Note: I am not suggesting that a dad figure is the only way you might have learned these things, but people I know have learned them from their dads.) As I think of all the dads I know, each small idea represents something to be carried on.

Dads often do not have as much time to get their messages and advice to us as they'd like, and sometimes they stop trying. But for the most part, dads want to teach us to carry on. And as hard as that can be at times, it is a gift that makes our lives richer, and us, wiser. That's what I think as I run on my woodland trail, with the dad-tree creaking hello in the wind. So carry on, I will.

Good for what ails you

Something delightful to me is having a rainy Saturday afternoon in June to do with as I please. What pleased me this week was having time to weed my garden.

This year I decided to try hard to maintain some order in my little plot of terraced garden facing the riverbank. Other years I'd start with the best of intentions in April or early May, right after the snow melts. I'd clean up winter residue, turn over soil surrounding my narcissus, grape hyacinths, and daffodils, and I'd be cheered by an appearance of order.

But if I turned my head, weeds would sprout, like so many wild ideas. If I forgot to allocate time for gardening, within a week or two, there would be no hope of taming the jungle that grows so happily, all by itself. Where I live, wilderness is not only imaginable, it is tangible, and part of the everyday landscape. If I let my garden go untended, chaos came, green and wild, and assumed ownership.

This year, I experimented with a plan: I would weed just a little bit, whenever I had five or ten minutes, and I'd see if that would help keep order.

I discovered that the plan works and gives much back for the effort, including wisdom.

So a Saturday rain day was ideal for weeding. The soil was loose; weeds came up willingly, roots sliding out with only the slightest tug. I was able to move patches of perennials and transplant them. Chives, daisies and oregano are now in places I want them to be, rather than where I'd allowed them to spread. I moved Sweet Williams and forget-me-nots, and pulled crab grass from every spot it flourished. Every new-growth raspberry stalk came out, for the tenth time this year already.

As I puttered, the rain came, on and off, alternating with swarms of blackflies and mosquitoes. Were it not for the utter joy at playing in rich, moist soil, I'd have run for the shelter of my couch and a book I'd just begun. But I was hooked on dirt, on smells of the earth, and a willingness of a garden to conform to my ideas.

I was as covered by cloth as I could be—bandana sprayed with bug dope, work gloves, turtleneck, sweatpants, socks—I felt as safe as

I could from the buzzing critters. I was a kid, and my playing was much more important and imaginative than a bunch of bugs flying around my head.

I'd come inside for a glass of water, and look at my dirt-streaked face in the mirror. A definitely happy face kept looking back at me. And when I'd walk back out I'd see progress, the new earth grinning at me in the rain.

While I sat in my newly uncovered brick walkway, I thought about weeding, about what it is and what it does. What it is, is a choosing. Some things I don't need in my garden. I don't want them, and they grow lots of other places, so eliminating them does no harm. Removing weeds frees up valuable space, allowing other plants to grow without unnecessary competition.

It is also space for space's sake, an emptiness to contrast with the beauty of chosen plants, like a white wall in a museum ready to hang an honored Van Gogh. Removing weeds from walkways brings the bricks back to view. A path once promised is suddenly returned.

As for what weeding does, I kept thinking about my life while I was bent over, assessing, pulling and thinking some more. How, now that I'm in the middle of it, I can see how much weeding could be done. How many paths could be cleared, how much of what is good and possible could be allowed to flourish with just a little regular attention, and avoidance of unnecessary competition? I could work on the ordinary clutter of my life.

I've been weeding my library of books, my closets of clothes, and my storage spaces of stuff I'll never need to look at again. I'd always thought about my accumulations as projects for my later years—for rainy days when I'm old, when I'd look through boxes of papers, or shelves of old books, and enjoy my memories and the act of weeding through nostalgia.

But the accumulations are stifling, just like an unweeded garden. No chance to run with a good idea, if it is buried in a pile of unread books. No place for growth in an overcrowded jungle of maybes or I-don't-knows, because I hadn't thought about it, or because there was too much stuff still to sort through. Too much unfinished business ties me to a past also in need of weeding.

So in spite of, or because of, the rain and biting insects, an incredibly rewarding day was spent clearing spaces in a little patch of earth outside my kitchen window. I'll work at it, this year, as often as I can, tugging dandelions and Indian paintbrush and raspberries from my daisies, delphiniums, azaleas, irises and lilies.

And I'll think about the paths of possibilities in my life, and the rubble in the way. Bit by bit, I'll keep weeding, grinning, and wiping my face with dirty hands as I find my way.

Summer camp

This morning I helped one of my sons as he packed for camp. We went through a last-minute hunt for sandals; we remembered towels; we forgot the toothbrush. Some clothes to be packed got soaked in yesterday's torrential rains, and a guest was using the extra pillows. It was a chaotic, but exciting gathering and anticipation.

For the past eleven years, summer camp has been part of our family's Adirondack experience. Our kids have been happily incorporated into a different family, for one, two, or even six weeks during their various summer vacations.

At first I was not happy losing my "job" as private head camp counselor at our personal summer camp—our home. I spent many hours planning Adirondack activities for my children and their friends, and our visitors, and their children, year after year. It was like camp, but it was not camp. We had fun, but when the kids went to bed, it was usually in their own bed, with no sense of alternate space. And we didn't hear *Taps* being gently played before dozing off, like most campers do.

The first Sunday I drove home to an empty house after dropping off my entire crew of boys many years ago, I felt as though someone had kicked me in the gut. The kids were happily settled in their cabins, with their name tags on, their counselors watching over them at the beginning of a wonderful week full of outdoor experience. I, on the other hand, sat on the couch in my now huge and quiet home and thought about the day in the not-too-distant future when they would all be off into their own interesting lives. My house would be huge and empty then, too. I would remember this moment. This was a future lesson for me.

What does summer camp do for kids? It has been my experience to watch children grow in a very short period of time because of camp experiences. Camp allows them to be who they are, or could be, without their "normal" definitions of family, friends, neighborhoods, social standing, or fitting in. They make new friends; they spend most of their time outdoors; they learn how to make things, how to swim, and how to sing for their supper. They go on hikes and have camp-fires at night. They bond with the people they share their week with,

117

and they bond with the natural world they live in daily. They also learn how to navigate the camp system, who to follow orders from, and what the rules are. They eat good food, they are proud of the stuff they make, and they do not watch television. They are independent of the lives they left behind, and they learn to be comfortable in that new mode.

Days fly by for campers, just as they do for camp counselors. Camp counselors are usually kids who have grown up with summers spent at summer camp. Counselors have learned how to responsibly watch over their charges, remembering being someone's charges once themselves. They learn how to teach something to kids, like nature, swimming, crafts or outdoor cooking. They learn how to help supervisory adults maintain camp, cleaning up cabins, washing dishes, and even making sure the bathrooms are clean. They learn the value of being a positive role model for younger folks, and most take that role quite seriously.

These two groups create a microculture within a larger Adirondack culture. The camp world is not overly populated with adults; it relies heavily on the budding maturity of young adult counselors, fantastic pine-tree-and-lake scenery, and pleasant summer weather to create a place where our kids try on roles of being independent young Adirondackers.

Sometimes it is hard for campers to leave that summer world and come home. Even though parents are eager to see their smiling faces come through the door, the kids have had to learn to say good-bye to great new friends, kind counselors and campfires. It is sometimes difficult and sad, but it's an extremely helpful life experience.

Time, and an adult life spent in academia, taught me what else summer camp did for kids. Going off to camp helps kids learn, in a gentle way, about going away from home. The experience is immensely helpful when explaining what going off to college can feel like. A new world awaits with few adults, a different-from-home bed, living with people you don't know, rules to learn, subjects to conquer, no home cooking, campfires to gather around, making new friends, talking for hours, and achieving independence. Camp is a mini-adventure in young lives, preparing them for larger adventures in later years. I know this because it happened to me when I was young, and it changed my life.

So on that day years ago, when I was amazed and stilled by the silence in my house, I began to learn about letting go. In the process,

I found something else: Freedom to go out and explore the Adirondacks without packing for the kids. All-day hikes were possible, as were long canoe rides, and very short trips to the grocery store. It was a delightful reward to balance my lonely moment on the couch. Now on Friday evenings, when my campers return, I start the washing machine as soon as I hear the car pull into the driveway, ready for a week's worth of dirty socks and towels. I see on their faces that they've learned what I remember. I only wish I could play *Taps* so they would know.

Uncharted territory

Off in search of patches of plump blueberries, I decided to let my inner gyroscope guide me in the forest this morning. During the past few weeks I'd noticed most blueberry bushes having no fruit on the branches whatsoever, probably due to the hot month when we had no rain. But I know where there are some bushes that would not have been exposed to the dry, hot days, and today I went exploring.

Trails I hike on in the woods are interconnected with older trails and old logging roads, which I used to tromp along a couple of decades ago. And somewhere inside of me is a clear memory imprint of my years of woods-wandering.

I'm lucky like that. I generally do not get lost in the woods, or on trails, or even on roads and highways when going places. I know where north, south, east and west are without a compass. And since I love and study maps so much, my mental computer guides me, without making a sound, when I'm orienting outside of my home.

So today I wandered in unfamiliar terrain, quite fascinated with my adventure and my goal. I found the plump blueberries within the first twenty minutes, large patches of bushes in moist earth, under a forest canopy. I gobbled as many as I could grab, grinning through the sweet blue juices.

Then I looked out at the terrain, triangulated with some hill, mountain and creek landmarks, and set off in search of a direct route to my familiar trail system. I walked down a well-kept logging road I hadn't walked on in 25 years. The familiarity was striking and I was comforted by confirmation that my inner gyroscope's memory was intact.

I passed a few routes off to the left or right, and didn't take them. Then suddenly I saw another road, splitting off my current path, and I knew it would take me where I needed to go. Something about the lay of the land, the rise of the hill, and the type of trees told me this place was the back side of a hill I see from the other side when I hiked on my regular trails.

So I hiked up to the crest, and grinned widely. Downhill I could see familiar patterns, an opening in the canopy over the distant pond, and yes, way down there, the familiar brown bark-covered trails of my ordinary days.

Viewing Barnum Pond

photo by Randy Lewis

Having the courage to blaze a new path was a rush of adrenaline for me on this quiet, end-of-summer morning. I thought about how often we do not have that courage, when life shines a light on a possible new configuration for us, and we shake our heads, tamely staying on a path we already know.

Moving through uncharted territory adds to our lives. We take in new information, and we test our inner resources (like my inner gyroscope), to gauge our mettle. And we end up with a bigger life, with more stories and more lessons learned.

Sure, there is a little fear, and a little insecurity. It's like taking a test. And like taking a test, you won't know how you do until you actually do it.

The end of summer is a time of transition. Some little kids will enter kindergarten, leaving the security of home and riding a big yellow school bus for that first ride. Other kids will enter middle school, and begin changing classes, getting up an hour earlier every day.

Some people will end their summer jobs and move on to different jobs, or go back to school, or move to a new town. Some older folks will pack up and move back to where winters are warmer and more hospitable.

A new batch of people will leave home for college for the first time, bravely venturing into an uncharted world, testing their mettle. And some families will reconfigure, adjusting to newly empty bedrooms, suddenly quiet telephones, and smaller grocery bills.

And when we look outside, Mother Nature will also adjust. Leaves will turn red and orange and yellow, and all the trails will look different. What will remain the same is our trust in our inner resources. We may not know what's around the bend, or over the hill, but we can learn and grow wiser for the learning.

Take the uncharted path one of these days. Trust what you know. And grab one of life's juicy berries along the way.

Light without power

Last week, I was taking a shower at about 5 a.m., with the bathroom window open. A warm early morning, it was humid outside. Over the noise of splashing water, I heard a huge sound outside the window, like a big airplane flying very low. I got out of the shower and toweled off, listening to this strange roar, seeming to come from the west, down the river valley where I live.

Quite suddenly, up came a wind, right into the open bathroom window, blowing fiercely, knocking over the plastic cup by the sink. I quickly shut the window, understanding the wild hurricane-like sound I had just heard, then POOF! The lights went out.

That wind was furious. I was not. After all, my shower was over, I didn't get caught with soapy hair, as has happened numerous times in the past, and I knew exactly how far I had to feel my way to reach the nearest flashlight. Having no power first thing in the graying morning is nowhere near as difficult to maneuver as when it happens in the dark of night. Making sure everyone had a flashlight by their beds, I was able to head out to work.

Navigating the road I live on was amazingly difficult. Wind had knocked trees and branches down, and millions of early autumn leaves came off their nubs. The road looked like a riotous party had gotten way out of hand. I got out of the car several times, pulling big branches off to one side or the other. I drove off the side of the road when logs were too big for a single person to heft. And I saw my neighbors out with chain saws, immediately trying to free us from the labyrinth created by Mother Nature. Chain saws don't need electricity to help us help ourselves.

Living out in isolated areas around our small towns, Adirondackers are accustomed to losing power on a fairly regular basis. I tell visitors that at least ten times a year, sometimes even more than once a month, we can expect the lights to go out.

City folks cringe when they hear that. My mother-in-law, bless her, used to think we were nuts to live where it was possible the television did not work for days on end!

So what makes us lose power? Wind. Lots of wind. And snow. Sometimes it doesn't take all that much snow, either. Definitely ice.

We all remember how the ice storm of 1998 made our lives interesting, challenging, tough, and a little bit fun.

These are hostile weather conditions we are talking about, and our power lines are vulnerable. Often, when a tree limb is bent, or breaking with bad weather, it rests on the power line before taking out the power. We have brownouts when that happens; lights dim, maybe they go off, then pop back on. We have a warning that it looks like we'll lose our lights soon.

At our house, that's usually all we need to know to move into survivor mode. We have our own ritual, as do most folks who live here, and it looks like this: First, fill up a couple of buckets with water, then fill up a couple of pans with water, then a couple of water bottles. If we still have power after all that, we race about, gathering candles, flashlights, lanterns, batteries and matches. Rarely do we have enough time to do all this, but sometimes we do.

If all we get to do is fill water containers, that's fine. We can't use our water pump when there is no power. No hand washing, no toilet flushing, no cups of tea, no dish washing, and no macaroni making, unless we have gathered water first.

Everyone knows where there is at least one working flashlight. Each person has one in his room, in case the power goes out when it is dark. Each person also has a candle. I feel strongly that light is power over the confusion of darkness.

When power goes out with no warning, we have to search for all these things in the dark. We have several gallons of bottled water handy and any one of us can find at least one flashlight in a pinch. We have a gas cooking stove, a kerosene room heater, and a woodstove to heat our house—none which require electricity. So we can cook and stay warm when the power goes out. We take an abiding comfort in this.

Our phone still works, even without power. And we live by a river, which stays open and flowing all year round. So we have access to water (for toilet flushing) if the storm lasts awhile. We have a battery bag, too. When a snowstorm comes to stay awhile, we grab our radio, and our battery bag, and we still know what is going on out in the rest of the world.

What is so bad about losing power? We look silly reaching for the light switch on the wall. We can't watch our favorite shows on a television, which has become an empty, shiny, glassy black box in the living room. When our hands get dirty, we have to look around for a

photo by Randy Lewis

Hauling water when
the power goes out

way to clean them up. We have to adjust how to brush our teeth. We usually can't go anywhere, because when there is no power, the weather is usually too hazardous for driving. We have to put our busy plans on hold, even when they include very important responsibilities. We gather in smaller spaces, usually within sight of one another. And we talk, gathered around some small version of light.

Without power, we are creative. We come to our senses about the bottom line. What is important, after all? Not the television show, not basketball practice, not cleaning the bathroom. We are important. And those who are near us, sharing the quiet, they are important. Being able to make a cup of tea, or build a fire, or listen to a radio show...these are important.

We can imagine life before all our conveniences, no matter how briefly we are without electric lights. We can play cards with one another by candlelight or pull out a scrabble board to play a game. We can pull out the chess pieces and set up a match, or find that book we haven't had time to finish, and relax by a lantern. We marvel at how successful we are at surviving, even if just for a few hours. This is a gift, even if it doesn't feel like one when it happens. Many times I have noticed a small letdown on people's faces when lights come blinking back on. Back to life as usual, busy and scattered. Sometimes we sigh.

Losing power is part of our culture here in the woods, part of our definition. All of us know that momentary gasp...and our own rituals to make the best of the darkness. We bring our own light of creativity, candles, and quiet companionship to these times. Just like in real life situations, when you feel powerless, or in the dark, remember your creative spirit, and the light you can bring. We can easily defeat the harshness of being without power, and prove over and over that we are capable northern survivors.

Fall frenzy

With the first day of autumn comes the equinox when briefly, daylight and darkness are equal. But the entire fall season we are settling in, with darkness winning the daily tug-o-war, rolling towards the solstice in December, when daylight starts tugging back. Temperatures are cooler, and soon our major killing frost will hit.

Adirondackers exhibit behaviors this time of year that meld with the changing climate. As I slowly bring in plants which have enjoyed their summer out-of-doors, I prune them, and transplant them into larger pots. This morning I worked with my plants while I was baking cookies. A warm oven took the chill off the cool house, and the cookies smelled sweet and delicious.

Most people turn their attention towards their homes and kitchens during this season. In other kitchens I know pickles are being canned, tomatoes preserved, relishes concocted, and dilly beans being put up. Some friends are freezing corn, making spaghetti sauces, and turning cucumbers into wonderful additions to this winter's meals. Something about the temperature differential, cool frosty weather outside contrasting with a toasty kitchen with steamy windows inside, invites respite and camaraderie.

I become a baker. Unabashed, I seek out zucchini for breads, apples for muffins, and veggies for vegetable pies. I'll whip up cookies and brownies at the drop of a hat, especially if my nose is red and my hands are cold from working outside.

Our family eats meals of yummy vegetable-laden soup, with fresh out-of-the-oven cornbread, several times in the fall. And when we roll out our cider press for our cider days, we also make applesauce, apple pies, apple crisp, apple muffins, and apple stew, glorious gifts from our dozen apple trees.

We also wash house windows, taking down screens and putting up storm windows. We know how long and dark the days will be. When the sun comes out in the white, icy winter, sometimes it feels like bathing in rays of summer, standing inside in front of a clean, sunny window.

We clean out the garden, harvesting the last of everything but carrots and parsnips, which can wait until after the frost. We make sure wood is piled close to the house, all ready for snowfall. We get the shovels down from their spot in the rafters, and put them in the corner by the front door.

We go to football games and soccer matches, and cheer loudly, often with the steam of our breath making clouds in the chilled air. We pull out our coats, hats, boots, and mittens, and we begin to use them.

I also plant spring bulbs. Some years I am so positive, I buy up to ten varieties of spring cheer, and spend a good weekend preparing the ground, weeding, and finding homes for the bright colors I want to see come spring.

Daffodils and narcissus are my favorites, blooming from early spring, with snow still on the ground, to late, when there are tulips up, too. Some smell so sweet you could faint with the jolt it gives you when you walk by. These yellows and golds and whites are so artistic against an old, graying backdrop of melting snow, they look like hope.

Tulips and hyacinths are also favorites, bringing startling color and fragrance to spring. This is hard to imagine when you are handling the small brown onion-like bulbs and rocklike corms. But bulb planting is an act of faith, something we should hold on to facing winter.

One of the last things to do, on the first night the weatherman says a killing frost is coming, is to harvest the last blooms of flowers. I go out, usually after dark, after I hear the weather forecast. I gather the remaining nasturtiums, and I am happy to say, there are usually more than four bouquets of them, all red and gold and yellow, smelling like sweet nirvana.

Gathering the remaining gladiolas, their long gorgeous stems with the first colorful buds open, in my arms, I bring them inside, searching for tall vases. Then I zip back out, and with scissors, cut the roses. If I have any dahlias, I pick them. Then I come inside, and put bouquets all around the house, to honor the beauty of the season, and extend their gifts for a few more days.

We keep ourselves busy, moving from summer to fall. We know what is coming, and that preparation makes it all okay. Animals are doing it too, just look at the jowls of those chipmunks! But it is different than the expansion of spring; it is the drawing in of autumn, the homing time, when it is mostly dark outside. And sitting in a warm kitchen with an apple pie coming out of the oven, with flowers in vases all around the house, well, it is just a different slice of heaven, its own reward for a job well done.

Indian summer

Standing outside over the weekend, wearing shorts, I chatted with a neighbor. I leaned on my shovel, knees dirty, hands muddy, and over my shoulder, clean clothes hanging on a clothesline billowed in an occasional breeze. When the breeze stopped, small flies appeared, hovering near our faces.

Snow was melting before our eyes, and there was a giddy sense of meteorological euphoria as we chatted. I could hear sounds of a staple gun from one nearby house, plastic being stapled on windows to close in a home before winter, to minimize heat loss during the impending cold. It's so much easier to do this stapling job when the air is warm.

Another neighbor transported one wheelbarrow load of firewood after another from an outdoor woodpile to an indoor one. Somewhere else windows were being washed. Carpentry projects were under way, the whining sounds of circular saws were punctuated by sharp hammering noises. Busy people were everywhere; you could just feel it.

One man raked old leaves which were becoming exposed by rapidly melting snow. I watched him pause and gaze out at a beautiful mountain view. He must have done that quiet glancing outward a thousand times, but this is one time when someone noticed him. Seeing deep appreciation in action is heartwarming and contagious.

After several weeks of early winter weather, we've been given a brief respite of late Indian summer. Since trees have mostly dropped their leaves, this warm, sunny time seems unnaturally bright and enchanting. We can suddenly see through the forests. We notice ridge lines of nearby hills and eskers, usually hidden by leaves on thousands of trees. We can step outside without hats and gloves for maybe just one more weekend. We know this is a rare gem, and it makes us happy.

I spent the weekend dirty and grinning. I'd regretted winter claiming us so early for a few reasons, the first being a hundred spring bulbs I'd not had time to plant before the snow fell. Fifty mixed daffodils and fifty multicolored iris bulbs taunted me from my back porch, labeling me "procrastinator" every time I walked by. Now, in the sun, Mother Nature had cracked open a door of opportunity which I was able to take advantage of.

I dug a ten-inch-deep hole about five feet wide on one side of my daffodil bed, and carefully placed the iris bulbs, pointed side up, in the hole. Then, like a happy puppy, I scraped cold brown soil back into the hole, putting the bulbs to sleep for the season. I did the same thing in the side yard for mixed daffodils. Finally, I was refreshed, rosy cheeked, and absolved of procrastinators' guilt all at the same time.

Then I made a few snowballs out of the receding snow, and practiced my throws, targeting a dead tree stump. I raked up some damp leaves, pruned some rose bushes, and looked closely at bright red berries on the shrubs, thrilled by the red song they sang. I threw a ball for the dog who hopped happily to retrieve it. Wind ruffled my hair, and I breathed in its softness.

Dry elm leaves crackled as they tumbled to the ground from their highest branches. On our property, the elm and apple trees are the last to let go, last leaves often landing on top of early snows. Today these fluttery leaves were all just a few loose golden November moments, but they were gifts in motion, memories of summer, brought on gentle spring-like breezes.

When this warm front arrived, we'd already had days of icy roads, snowy mornings and scraping windshields. I listened to people talking in the grocery store line, and at the gas station. We grumbled amongst ourselves: "This is too soon," and "I wasn't finished with fall chores yet." We made appointments for getting the snow tires put on, grabbed shovels, and kept moving forward. We know the drill. We are survivors in the great north woods.

Anticipating the weather change yesterday, I looked out my window and saw a single white moth fluttering its wings. I do not know the lifespan of such a fragile creature, but I do know what it looks like to make the best of your lot in life. Here was a single moth, flapping papery wings on a rare, beautiful near-winter day, without another bug anywhere in sight. This was its one shot at a life. There was spirit in that vision, and a message.

We all should learn to grab the moment and make it be something that matters. Life is generally full of lists, plans and responsibilities, often peppered with moments of regret. Some of us are burdened by more regret than others, and it can blind us from appreciating the natural healing gifts we've been offered in quiet ways.

These are things I learned: When you're suddenly struck by a feeling of good luck, or something sweet happens, like a totally unexpected warm day deep in November, try to breathe it in. Go out in it, let it touch your face, and smile. Recognize the value of what you've been given. When it feels like your time for happiness, accept it. Do something to avoid the future dull ache of regret. Turn a could've, should've, or would've into an act of accomplishment. Be bold about it.

Regret, like anger, is an unhealthy condition. When used properly, as motivation, it can create positive change. But when constant and unresolved, it can make you sick. So don't choose to live a life of regret. Even if you're the only papery white moth in town, and it's after a snowstorm in the middle of November, get out there and give it all you've got. Grab your moment and fly with it. You just may be an inspiration to us all.

Keeping warm

The sky is a brilliant blue, with a couple of big puffy white clouds floating lazily overhead. The sun is so bright that I'm squinting indoors. All the trees outside are adorned with diamonds of ice, twinkling in captured sunlight.

It is extremely cold outside in that sunlight. Local weather stations say one thing for other area communities, and something completely different for ours. We're just plain colder. We take a strange pride being recognized as the coldest spot in the nation, which we are from time to time. We're cold weather folks, and even if we don't like it, we have found our ways not only to survive, but also to find comfort in that survival.

Our house has been carefully constructed over the past couple decades with close attention paid to enduring cold weather. We have super insulation, R19 in the walls, R40 in the ceilings. We have thermal pane windows, and lots of them. The south side of the house alone has 19 windows, which allow lots of sunlight in, all winter long. On a frigid sunny day like this, the whole house is warmed by the winter sun. It can even become too warm, especially if you're sitting in a chair with the sun heating up your body.

As a young family, tied close to home by babies and toddlers, we heated our house only with wood. We bought an excellent woodstove, which, once full of wood, could heat us well for over eight hours, and lingering heat could keep us warm longer than that.

Families with little kids generally don't do a lot of recreational travel, so only heating with wood for a few years suited us just fine. But once the boys got big enough to go on journeys with us, we decided to add some backup heating so the pipes wouldn't freeze if we couldn't find a neighbor to keep a wood fire burning.

We bought electric heating units for a few rooms in the house, especially the bathrooms. We wired the other rooms so we could add electric units to them in the future. Then, suddenly liberated, we were able to leave town for a whole weekend at a time. With young children, practicality set in. After all, we just wanted to visit grandparents or friends in central New York. With our new backup heat, we could finally leave.

A few years later, we rebuilt the kitchen half of the house. We changed a tiny dark kitchen and attached garage into a large, bright, eat-in kitchen area. Our new space immediately quelled the dark forces of winter gloom. The windows let in daylight, and the beauty of surrounding woods came right into the room. This new space also became much colder on frigid winter days and nights than the smaller, cramped kitchen we'd dismantled.

So we bought a nice-sized, backup propane room heater for the chilly kitchen area. This heater kicks on during real cold weather, working even when the power has gone out. After that installation, our little family was able to leave for up to a week at a time which we did, happily, during cold times.

Every year we'd try to find somewhere warmer to go during the deepest cold times. It was nice to have a little oasis of time to let down our guard. It was nice not needing hats, mittens, scarves, snow-suits, jackets, vests and boots for each boy, JUST TO GO OUT TO THE CAR! Families with a handful of little kids know what a relief it is, just to have a small break in that incredibly time-consuming proce-dure of dressing and undressing youngsters for the winter elements every single day.

With our backup heat and kindly neighbors willing to toss wood into the woodstove, we were free to go soak up some milder climate. Usually we headed to Florida, to visit grandparents and friends, but we also went to South Carolina and Oregon, places without snow. We enjoyed ourselves and the break in the routine, and relaxed, knowing our home would be just fine without our constant care.

Now that the kids are out of the house, we're thinking of getting a furnace. Furnaces are not familiar to me, but I know many people have them, and rely on them year after year. I hear you just turn a knob on a wall somewhere, and some miracle of warmth occurs. You don't have to lift, split, carry or pile anything at all with a furnace, I'm told. And there are no wood chips or ashes or mounds of dust to consider, either.

My grandparents' houses had furnaces. Big bulky appliances hid-den in the dark recesses of old cellars, furnaces were places young-sters were told to stay away from. Kids are naturally fascinated with anything they are told to stay away from. I remember being drawn to the furnace, looking at a small flicker of flame through a big iron door, and wondering if it were magic, or if I could die if I touched it.

By the time I'm a grandparent, perhaps I'll have those same cautionary lines to say to my grandchildren, who might be prowling around, exploring this big house. I suspect that having a furnace makes winter life in the north woods easier. Maybe I've put enough hard time in, years of lugging wood, stacking wood, removing splinters from my hands, and cleaning woodstoves. Now it's time to enjoy some magic warmth; maybe I've earned this. Or maybe I'll be spending the coldest time of the year somewhere warmer, or snowless, waiting for a visit from youngsters who will themselves be living somewhere where their parents are heating with wood.

In either case, and until then, I've got to clean out the ashes, get some kindling and wood, and load the stove now. I hear it's going to be ten below tonight.

Thirty three below

One recent day when we woke up early to a temperature of thirty three below zero, we were also bestowed with the gift of a bright full moon, casting long, deep shadows on the snow in the morning darkness. It makes sense, of course, that the coldest nights are cloudless. Cloudlessness allows the small amount of heat which may have built up during the day to escape into the cold universe, without earth's protective cloud layer to hold it in.

Weathermen tell us that all the time. They also say, "Boy, it's going to be a cold one tonight!" or, as I heard yesterday, "If you think this was cold, just wait until you see what's heading our way in the upcoming week. Coming right up, our five-day forecast."

The Weather Channel reported most major eastern cities were reaching the coldest temperatures they'd experienced in three years. Those cold temperatures were balmy compared with our own. Who can feel sorry for folks in New York and Boston struggling with 15-degree temps when our frigid, unforgiving air struggled and repeatedly failed to make it up to zero?

I will not overlook a very important factor in survival stories of North Country winter living. We just don't complain all that much about the cold. Who would we complain to? We're in this act together, after all.

Channel 5 news crews from Plattsburgh came to town to interview some Saranac Lake locals about their take on living in such a cold place, at such a cold time of the year. When the piece aired that evening, the newscasters were amazed that we Tri-Lakers mostly don't fuss about the frigid time of year. In fact, what they laughed at was this: We really didn't think it was all that cold. "This is not so bad, really," an interviewee said, while the poor reporter shivered visibly holding the microphone.

Another person said, "It is so beautiful when it's bitter cold." I totally agree: Some crystalline panoramic views just take your breath away when the air is crispy, the sun is bright, and temps are below zero.

"I like it cold like this," said another resident. "This is why we live up here."

What exactly does it feel like, when it is a couple dozen degrees below zero? I've asked several people lately, to see what their senses have told them, and this is what they've said:

• Your nose freezes. Sometimes it sticks to the inside of itself, and often it gets bright red. (When you come back inside, it definitely begins to melt and drip.)

• Your skin feels brittle, as though a big smile just might crack it into pieces and make it bleed.

• Air entering your lungs feels tight and foreign, as though taking a deep breath would hurt.

• Fingertips and toes get cold quickly. Sometimes they get extremely cold, and they throb in rhythm with your heartbeat. Then they really hurt.

• Eyelashes feel like they carry frozen tears. Eyeballs feel dry, and blinking is an act you can actually feel, a little like sandpaper on skin.

• If your teeth are exposed to the weather, they are sensitive, and you can imagine them freezing and breaking off.

• If you go out without long johns, your legs get icy, and you can feel your pants scratch on the tender skin. If you do wear long johns, it just takes a little longer for this sensation.

• Your hair freezes around the edges of your hat, making little icicles you can barely feel since your skin is nearly ice itself.

When we first arrive here from less frigid places, we quickly learn about the joys of wool and the sensibility of dressing in layers. Wearing vests and sweaters and turtle necks, we are always more confident with our long johns on. We learn to know enough to keep our feet warm. Good, warm socks are magic elixir for those spending time outdoors.

So are good boots. A friendly face stopped me in town one day last week, noticing my non-boot footwear. She chastised me, good naturedly, for not having boots on, with steamy breath coming out her mouth, over the top of her scarf, as she spoke.

We chatted about the benefits of boots, and the sorrow at getting holes in my last good pair last year. As we parted, she said, "Now go get yourself some good boots and keep yourself warm, okay?" and we both laughed. I knew she cared, but I also knew I couldn't afford a new pair this year. I wasn't going to tell her that. She'd probably find me a pair somewhere to get me through the tail end of the season. Plus, I had a great scarf and hat and new mittens, so I knew I'd make it through the end of the winter okay.

Without this coldness, folks in Saranac Lake would have quite a bit of trouble building our annual Winter Carnival Ice Palace. This year, our world famous crystalline architectural masterpiece is going up quickly and beautifully, rising tier by tier from the shores of Lake Flower, a testament to our wacky partnership with the cold. Smiling faces are out there, people grinning and working hard to assemble this huge palace from giant blocks of frozen lake water, thirty below or not. Some people just don't get it; they think we're nuts.

So we move about our days in the strange complicity of frigid air and community. We've been given the gift of seeing the magic of a big white moon, and the long and sinewy dark shadows cast upon the sparkling snow during these nights of frozen air. We stoke our fires and know that we're the real residents of the Adirondacks, true winter survivors, and we're doggone proud of it.

Rituals of winter

On this, the twelfth day of Christmas, we make time to clean up the remnants of the holiday season and settle in with our other winter rituals.

Those of us with Christmas trees usually have them undecorated by now, with ornaments and lights put away until next December. I'm always happy to return the tree to the outdoors. So is the tree.

Ritual with tree

This is my ritual:

I examine the tree carefully for remaining tinsel or hidden ornaments, unscrew it from its base, then lug it unceremoniously through the kitchen, then the back porch, until I get it outside to the backyard. This lugging is not easy; a tree most assuredly is an awkward houseguest, with outstretched limbs, and thousands of tiny needles dropping as branches smack against door jambs on the return journey to the woods.

But once outside, the little tree has come home. I find a spot near my bird-feeding station, and carefully put its trunk deep into a pile of snow.

Once again those balsam branches move in the wind, and small birds light on them, as they wait to eat at feeders. When snow falls on this little tree, Mother Nature performs a calm and excellent job of decorating while snow clings to its outstretched branches once again.

Ritual with shovel

Other winter rituals are abundant and noticeable after the holidays. They include shoveling snow, feeding birds, shoveling snow, going for walks, shoveling snow off the roof, going to basketball and hockey games, brushing snow off car windows, skiing, sledding, snowshoeing, ice skating, snowboarding, and of course, shoveling snow some more.

Even folks with snowblowers and small snowplows have to shovel a little snow, so owning at least one snow shovel seems to be an Adirondack common denominator. We have at least six shovels, many weights and sizes, collected over the years.

137

After decades of life in the North Country, we have learned about shoveling snow. One thing I've learned is that I enjoy it. I've always been pretty warm blooded, and generally I am out there shedding my hat and gloves after a few minutes of hearty activity.

Step by step

Here's my shoveling routine:

After a big snowfall, I grab the widest shovel, which is stored right by the front porch door in the winter, and shovel off the front steps. Then I begin to make the first path to the driveway, then on out to the road. I put the shovel down through the snow to the hard surface below, and just begin pushing. By the time I get to the road, I no longer feel snowbound. I turn around and widen the path as I return to the porch.

Next I grab a smaller-width shovel and begin clearing the walkway to the front door, now lifting and tossing the snow which no longer has room to be pushed aside.

Once the sidewalk is done, I begin a different pattern of shoveling when I get to the driveway. I begin by tackling the biggest roadside piles of snow where the snowplow, if it has been by, has deposited all the road snow. This snow is heavy, sandy, chunky, and deeper than the rest of the newly fallen crystalline precipitation. It has to be moved from the driveway, often over high snowbanks, in order to get cars out.

Advice to avoid pain

By this time, the physical workout of shoveling is well under way. I'm usually rosy cheeked, with snow melting in my hair. I've developed a rhythm of pushing piles, lifting and tossing, which incorporates as much "sensible" physical know-how as possible.

Keep your knees bent. Use your arm and shoulder muscles instead of your back. Push whenever possible, instead of lifting. Switch sides. If you don't, it will cause serious imbalance in your structure. And whatever happens, don't jerk and twist at the same time. Lifting a heavy load and turning to toss it over a snowbank has landed many shovelers in local chiropractors' offices or in massage therapy every winter. (Plus it hurts.)

After the big snowplow pile at the end of the driveway has been cleared, I make smaller, manageable squares of the rest of the driveway, and finish them off until the job is done, much the same way I

photo by Randy Lewis

One family's shovels, ready for action

tackle mowing lawns in the summer, geometrically. I always take a moment to enjoy the quiet, gentle muffle of a world covered in snow. Thoughts abound as I work.

I'll finish up this job, all sweaty and happy, and come inside, ready for some hot tea. Generally this is the time when the town snowplow will come by again, plowing up another small snowbank at the end of my cleared driveway, but that perennial irony is part of the humor of this ordeal.

Universal ties

Everyone has their own shoveling rituals. I drove through the residential areas of Saranac Lake after a recent snowfall, looking at everyone outside shoveling. All types of shovels were being used and all ages of residents were out there shoveling. Both genders were represented, it didn't matter. All lengths of driveways and walkways were being freed from their snowy blankets. The process seemed quite neighborly, and universal.

We're united as we make our way through piles of snow every winter. We're united in a way that folks in Miami or San Diego probably cannot even imagine. We live where snow comes, white and deep, offering us a chance to engineer our paths to civilization with the tools of winter at hand, a true common denominator of an actively Adirondack life.

Road warriors

The culture of our northern communities demands to include our vehicles. This time of year is particularly hard on all of our cars and trucks, believe me.

One day this week I walked down the streets of Saranac Lake, looking at cars parked alongside the street. They all sported a dusty, dirty, dry coating. I'd never before noticed the universality of the tired-looking condition.

Every single car had a layer of gray, white, and brown splatter, from windows down to tires. Some were spattered and coated on the windows, too. Caked-on salt, dried puddle water, and frozen slush all adhered to once-shiny surfaces.

In my own vehicles, this spat-out stuff also creeps into door mechanisms and suspension areas, making loud groaning and creaking metal a familiar sound to my late-winter ears.

Cars are so vital to our mountain lifestyles, we can't do without them. Our transition season of late winter-early spring is the harshest environment for our metal steeds.

Ever wonder about the geological phenomenon of frost heaves? Frost heaves are surprising rutted road conditions North Country people encounter this time of year. After looking up information in books, and online, I've asked area smart people for their input, yet still remain a little unsure about the big WHY of it all.

The ground we live and walk upon is earth constructed of different-sized particles which are made up of many different materials. Water, and later ice made from that water, fills the spaces between these soil particles, expanding and contracting with variations in temperature. This expanding and contracting water and ice move the earth particles located around the ice, whether the soil's surface has a road on top of it or not.

Predictably, year after year in northern climates, deep dips form in road surfaces in January, when the earth below has been shifted by Mother Nature. Those wavy dips stay until April or May when temperature extremes are moderated. So all of us vehicle drivers ought to be tooling down our familiar roadways with a little more caution, once we've been startled by the first unexpected head-bumping, shock-crunching introduction to frost-heave season.

Ask your car how it enjoys those surprises!

And potholes? They appear mysteriously overnight. Wide, deep, gaping holes exist where just the day before was smooth road surface. If a driver is not alert, the poor vehicle bumps over or into the hole, sometimes sending wheel alignment to never-neverland.

After a rough experience like that, the poor car shakes and rattles until you can take it to your busy car doctor for repair.

Another surprise for our cars and trucks is a living thing. Deer are on the move this time of year, hungry, and looking for food. They move through their winter environment, crossing roads without a second thought, and definitely without caution lights for unsuspecting drivers. The hooved beasts usually travel in multiples, so one deer seen crossing a road often means there is another one close behind. Most deer run when they are moving through those open spaces, innocently unaware of the speed of an upcoming vehicle, or the consequences of a collision.

Those collisions can be astounding. Almost every driver I know has collided with at least one deer, and some more than one. Thousands of dollars of damage can be caused to your trusty car as it violently bumps into fast-moving, 200 pounds of wild animal. One neighbor's new car was completely totaled a couple of years ago. We won't mention the damage suffered by the animal, or the emotional toll of the violent encounter on the driver, but both are heady. There is no way to predict these meetings, except to say they could and do happen to anyone.

So this really is a season of endurance for our cars and trucks. With weather fluctuations and surprises abounding, drivers can experience slush, black ice, snow, and unexpected encounters with deer on a regular basis. Our brakes need to work dependably; our windshield washer fluid must be full, our wipers functional, and our eyes alert to changes in familiar road surfaces.

The angle of the sun is changing, too, along with the hours of sunrise and sunset. So at this time of year our commute might be at times when we are blinded by direct sun. Factor this into the driving formula, and we have challenging experiences, along with a cornucopia of potentially dangerous variables to navigate through in our everyday travels.

This truth is universal up here in the north woods.

So be kind to your vehicles. Drive more cautiously. Take your buddy to the car wash once in a while. Keep sunglasses handy. Watch out for the late winter wrinkles in the earth we must drive on. Your cars and trucks will thank you.

Then, before you know it, it will be spring.

Tax time and picnics

April 15 is a date that often scares people, especially procrastinators. Income tax day comes faithfully year after year, just like spring. We all have to abide by the rules, do what we're told, fill out the forms. Tax forms are unquestionably difficult to understand, and the process of collecting forms, reading directions, filling in empty boxes with numbers derived from computations on other forms, and getting these things in the mail on time always takes some planning, organizational skills and time.

If you've got those skills, and the time, it is merely a duty that you complete. If you don't, you wear your procrastination like an extra heavy coat on a warm day and you look around for others similarly hot under the collar.

My forms were in the mail a week earlier than usual this year. This relief feels wonderful, and offers me time to look out at the rest of my April environment without the awful preoccupation and stress of tax procrastination.

What do I see this Easter Sunday? I see snow melting, ice thawing and robins everywhere, laughing.

Neighbors held an annual Easter brunch outdoors, not too far away, but far, far from civilization. The setting was ideal, right next to a mid-sized pond undergoing its big spring melt.

Everyone brought a dish to share with other guests. Our menu looked like this: hot coffee, orange juice, champagne, beer, pineapple chunks, melon wedges, blueberries, grapes, frozen strawberries (for the champagne), raspberries, a raw vegetable platter with spinach dip, an Easter pie with bacon and eggs, an egg pie, bacon slices, a spicy potato dish, a noodle kugel, fresh breads, and a delicious maple-pear upside down cake. All dishes were nicely displayed on a picnic table, with a pot of blooming tulips grinning nearby.

Adirondack chairs and comfortable folding chairs faced bright midday sun and the thawing pond. Overhead, while we watched, an adult osprey hovered, definitely spying a meal in open water below. He would soar, then return to hover, raising our expectation of a diving performance. Then he would shift and soar again.

We sat in chairs outside, eating, then raising our faces, lifting them, eyes closed, like pale plates hungry for rays of sun. Not a cloud marred the sky. People spoke quietly and cheerfully to one another, basking in the beauty of the day, and the satisfaction of a great meal. Out on the pond, a very large chunk of ice detached from the mass. It floated on a slow current, towards more open water, a disintegration of one symbol of winter. We talked about how some years we sit and watch otters as they play in open holes in the ice. Dark and frisky, they bob their heads up through emerging holes, and play peek-a-boo with Mother Nature.

From afar we saw a flock of snow geese in the sky. Their noticeable vee-formation would catch the glint of sun, illuminating them briefly, then they would vanish as their wings tilted to a different angle, an optical illusion in the heavens.

A few times groups of ducks would land on the open water, float around for a while, then take off noisily. Songbirds were hiding in the trees; unable to be silent in all that sun, they told us who they were by their songs.

Easter is the time of year when some of us think about the words resurrection and renewal. "Bringing back to life" is exactly what is happening right now. One by one the threads that bound us in winter's grip are unraveling. The process takes awhile, but steps in the resurrection of our forest world are familiar, year after year.

Watching patches of earth appear in snowy lawns and fields is a miracle. Slow enough to capture our sense of wonder, they balloon into pastures of readiness. We find treasures as the world of color awakens. Yesterday I found my watering can when the snowbank covering it melted down enough to show its green pouring arm extended, waving hello. A bright green cocktail napkin blossomed as my driveway melted. Earth underneath the trees is littered with fallen branches of every size. Treasures stolen by winter are now soggily returned.

Crocuses have been sighted in many places. Two purple blossoms bloomed in my backyard today. Making it through winter still alive, they are able to sing their bright song. Daffodils and narcissus have pointy greenery jutting up through residual snow and last autumn's leaves. They are small plants, powerfully reaching upward, toward light, toward the mighty sun. Their green color in dark, damp duff is full of hope and promise. Their unfolding blossoms will dazzle even the most winter-weary among us, when it is time.

Rivers and streams swell with snowmelt, and make a bigger sound, moving jauntily through their beds. Wet earth, newly emerged, smells rich and musty, anticipating growth, ready to get the show on the road.

April can represent a return to the senses: sights, sounds, and smells all coming back, reborn every spring. The white of winter is calming, and quiet, but blankets all the life we welcome back on the wings of an osprey, or open petals of purple crocus blossoms.

Snow will fall again, but will also thaw quickly. Ice chunks will continue breaking off, otters will play, and once-still waters will open wide. Birds will keep making their nests, and days will grow longer and longer. April 15 next year is a long way off, and we have another whole cycle of life in the mountains to enjoy in the meantime.

Chapter 4

Three Views of Black Bears

Suddenly there was a loud noise

you were sitting on the bed
reading Edward Abbey
I was lying next to you
reading Raymond Carver
it was late and dark
suddenly there was a loud noise
outside the open window
the garbage can knocked over again
I said maybe a bear this time?
you said I doubt it
I handed you the flashlight
you went into the night
to check it out
and I haven't seen you
since
the cat is meowing
chasing moths that bounce their heads
against the screens
the children are all asleep
it is summer
we are both forty
but not for long.
please come back.
we're just getting
to the good part.

(Previously printed in *Blueline 17*, 1996, and *The Blueline Anthology*, Syracuse University Press, 2004)

Close encounters: Running bear

After a busy week, I was happy to grab my hiking poles to head into the woods yesterday morning. It was about 54 degrees and misty, sometimes breaking into a gentle rain. But I relished this unencumbered time.

Usually, I hike quickly halfway through my trail route, then I run the second half, after I'm all warmed up. If I get caught up with thinking or observing, I sometimes forget to run. I've learned not to let that bother me.

A little ways into the forest in the mist, I noticed a black bulky figure way ahead to one side of the trail. I'd never seen a bear in this section of the woods, so I wondered if maybe it was just that. Instead I saw it was merely a darkened tree stump as I got closer, then passed it by, relieved.

Because of my little list of stresses from the week, I wasn't paying close attention to the beautiful natural world around me. So I stopped and plucked my very first summer blueberry. I decided to empty my head of problems I couldn't solve.

That berry was sweet, plump and wildly juicy. Just yesterday I'd picked a wild red strawberry, and I knew raspberries were soon to follow.

I started running, with even steps and a beating heart playing rhythm to the foot-beats on the trail.

I stopped at the waterfalls and raised my poles to the sky in gratitude for my wonderful misty morning. As I continued my run, I rounded a bend, and in a microsecond noticed another black bulky figure by the side of the trail, about 30 feet away.

This time it moved.

The difference between a darkened tree stump and a bear starts with its shiny eyes, followed quickly by the untamed brain behind it. And then there's the snout, which snorts.

This large, black mammal was just as startled by me as I was by him. He looked at me, made a harumphing noise, and quickly ran off into the woods, making a ton of noise, squashing ferns and underbrush, and breaking twigs as he rumbled away. He looked over his shoulder at me just once, and kept going.

He was not a full-sized bear, I noticed immediately. I'd guess he was a yearling, about the size of a large, filled-out St. Bernard. I'd say he was at least 175 pounds, by the sound he made lumbering away, but that's just a guess.

But I wondered, all in the microsecond of encounter, how long does a mother bear worry about her kid? Six months? A year?

So I lifted my poles, spoke quickly and loudly, "I'm outta here!!!!" and began backtracking, going in the opposite direction from my new friend *Ursus americanus.*

I ran off the trail through the brush and on to an old abandoned logging road I knew led to the closest paved road, about a half mile away.

Then I began to run for my life (or so I thought).

All my running years, nearly 30 of them, I'd wondered if my training would ever help me out in a pinch. I'd imagine a scene from a movie, running down a city street at night, away from some bad guy. Or I'd imagine being a messenger with a life-or-death message that I'd be responsible for running across the prairie, maybe with a posse after me.

I always thought how glad I'd be to be a true runner, with thousands of miles under my belt. Here's how it really felt:

I'm running down this soggy logging road, with sandy spots, rocky spots, and flooded spots along the way. Wet, knee-high grass interspersed with holes filled with water and mud, and bush limbs jutting into the path—all defied my pace.

I'm running as fast as I can, my poles getting caught in twigs pulling me backward, my running shoes filling up with water, my legs getting soaked. My heart is beating fast, and my empty head is listening for pounding bear foot-beats behind me.

Scared and exhilarated at the same time, I am pretty darn slow for being thrust into a legitimate running emergency. I'm in a dream, I'm panting, I'm worried, and I think maybe I'm crazy.

I am out at the road, and begin a wet, forlorn walk, way back to my car. I stop quite often for a ripe blueberry, and my steps are squishy, laden with puddle water. I regain my breath and composure, and wonder where the bear is right this moment. Finally I am me again.

When I got home, I grabbed my Peterson's *Field Guide to Mammals.* This is what I learned.

The black bear is the commonest and most widely distributed bear species. Usually nocturnal, they sometimes wander about in the daytime. They eat berries (a lightbulb moment), nuts, tubers, insects, small mammals, eggs, carrion and garbage. They have poor sight, moderate hearing and a good sense of smell. They can live 30 years or more and have a litter of cubs every other year.

Black bears may stay with their mother for one year (another lightbulb moment).

This is the family of largest living carnivores, and it dates from the Middle Miocene era, as noted by fossils left behind. These black furry creatures have a longer and more legitimate claim to the north woods than I do.

I've seen bears at least a dozen times in the past couple of decades. This was the closest encounter without the protection of a house window or car. I usually call it "a bear year" if I've seen one. I feel the bear spirit when my eyes actually take in the black fur, the huge paws, and those wild dark eyes. It is scary and very lucky to be near the animal heart of the mountains.

It was also the most exciting encounter I'd had, since in retreat, I, too, became a wild animal in the woods, running my heart out in the morning mist.

And we both got to pick plump berries in the forest as our juicy reward.

Threshold 2004

Standing on the deck of a little cabin nestled in the redwoods of northern California, I heard my cell phone ringing inside. My friend, Cynthia, was on her own cell phone in the next cabin, talking to a real estate broker about an offer she'd placed on a house in nearby Crescent City. I could hear the excitement in her voice.

We had each been looking at houses out here, thinking of the possibility of moving to this wonderland of ocean, fog, redwoods and big rivers. Houses were expensive, but not as expensive as they were in the rest of California. It seemed to be a good time to consider investing, before the prices skyrocketed, according to Cynthia. It was a time in our lives to fantasize about living somewhere else besides the mountains of northern New York, or the desert in southern Nevada. She was a lot more ready to leap than I was, however. For her it was high summer in the desert, with daily averages hovering around an inhuman 109.

For me, it was just July, with too many tourists and deerflies to be completely happy.

I finally found my own phone, ringing under a suitcase, and said, "Hello?"

There was a lot of static, a crunchy kind of electrical sound that drives cell phone users crazy.

"Hi Randy, can you hear me?" said the voice on the other end. "(Hiss, scratch, crackle) It's Debbie." Debbie is my neighbor back home.

I walked to a different spot on the deck, and said, "Hi Debbie, sorry for the bad reception. I can sort of hear you now. What's up?"

"Well, Randy, I have sort of bad news for you. It would help if I knew you could hear me. A bear broke into your house last night. (Hiss, crackle, scratch)..."

"Wow, really?" I said, hoping to improve the phone's reception by pointing my face toward the sky.

"Yeah, it's not good. It looks like he got stuck inside and tried to smash his way out, (hsss, scratch crackle)..."

"What??? Can you hear me? Debbie???"

"Well, Randy, there are a lot of broken windows, lots of broken plants. The good news is he didn't do too much damage in the bathrooms. But he broke your back door off, some walls are seriously damaged, there's bear shit everywhere, and lots of blood, and I can't find your cats. I am so sorry, (hiss crackle, scratch)..."

"Debbie? Debbie?"

"(hiss, crackle)...even upstairs, and there are so many people here right now, it's such a mess...(hiss, crackle hiss)..."

"What do you mean 'so many people?' Can you find my cats? Debbie? Can you hear me?"

I looked down at the phone and it said "disconnected."

I felt a little shaky. I looked up at the towering redwoods. The very tops of the trees were in the fog. It was a quiet morning, about 8:30, which meant that back home in my house in the Adirondacks it was about 11:30, and when I thought about it, the day was Friday. Everything in the world was different than it had been just a few minutes ago. Right now was the beginning of "after." I looked up at the tall trees again, and reconsidered that thought. For an ancient redwood, around for hundreds and hundreds of years, this was not even a missed beat. I took a deep breath.

Suddenly Cynthia came running over, full of joy. "I got the house! I got the house! I'm not stuck in the desert anymore!"

I wanted to make a reservation to fly home that very day. But where I was, in the beautiful isolation of the north Pacific coast, there were absolutely no airports close by. We were scheduled to fly home in seven days, and realistically could not leave early.

My cats. I kept thinking about my cats. Those poor old feline ladies who'd shared the past 15 years with me must be totally freaked out, or even dead, I thought. My house. My handmade house, which we'd been building and working on slowly and methodically for over 20 years, had been violated by a wild beast. And I hadn't been there to protect it.

Bears. We see them all the time in the Adirondacks; practically every year we have one sort of encounter or another. I remember the first time, my very first year of living in my house in the woods. I was pregnant, happy, and newly married. One night I went to the bathroom to close the bathroom window and looked outside. There was a big black bear, just being there on the other side of the window. Then he stood up and faced me, about five feet from my own face. I immediately realized that meant he was pretty tall, since I was inside, standing in the bathtub and he was out there, standing on the ground. We

153

were eye to eye. I was amazed before I became frightened. I slammed the window closed, and then slammed the bathroom door behind me as I sought the sanctuary of the middle of the house. Living here would be exciting, I thought back then, when it was all new.

Other encounters included me seeing a mother bear and a cub while I was out walking my newborn son the following summer. The two bears were about a quarter mile down the road, out walking, just like me. I turned the stroller around and ran my heart out to get back to my house. That time I was really afraid for the safety of my child, feeling like a protective mother animal myself, ready for battle if necessary.

Usually the bears who come are after our garbage or compost or birdfeeders. We would hear stories about neighbors having close encounters, sometimes with a bear breaking into their homes. One friend had a bear break into their newly remodeled kitchen. It destroyed the entire room, pulling the refrigerator over, breaking every cupboard door and every single plate and glass they owned. It also was stupid enough to come back, after the humans had returned, only to face the ire of a raging Irishman with a rifle.

Another friend had to kill a bear which had broken into their back porch. Our friend sat on the other side of his back door on his stairs with his gun. As soon as the bear crashed through that door, the rifle cracked, and that episode was over. Except for the cleaning up, of course.

Cleaning up. Oh, my. What was going to be in store for us, I wondered.

With terrible cell phone reception all day long, we finally managed to speak to people who could tell us what the damage looked like. Someone made a video of the entire scene, including the chaos of discovery of every single room's damage. One good friend after another told us what they saw. One of my sons went home from the city to call us, walking from room to room, telling us what was destroyed, and what was salvageable. Every room had suffered some damage, except the bathroom. My bedroom was the worst, hands down. My sanctuary, compromised. Someone finally found the cats hiding under a bed.

Someone else found a big empty bag of peanuts in the side yard, surrounded by peanut shells.

A neighbor came in and nailed plywood over the windows that were broken all the way through. He called and said, "Don't worry.

Everything is under control. We'll get someone to clean up the glass at least. Enjoy the rest of your vacation." This was much easier said than done.

Flash forward to the flight home.

I'm a regular flier. I love to fly. But this time I was haunted by the scenes of my home that my imagination had created. My poor old cats. My destroyed house. A battle zone between man and nature, all waiting for me when I rolled in. I couldn't doze or concentrate on the book I was reading. Every spot of turbulence made me nervous.

When the last plane finally landed, it landed abruptly, shocking all of the people in the cabin. We all made eye contact with one another in mutual relief as the plane rolled toward the gate.

Relief was my goal for the day.

The baggage took over 45 minutes to arrive at the baggage claim area. The conveyer belt was broken, people were frazzled, babies were crying, police were walking around, guarding against terror. It was 10:45 at night at the end of a very long, transcontinental day. I'd had breakfast in a coffeeshop in Portland, Oregon at dawn. We stopped at McDonald's in Burlington, Vermont, for supper 12 hours later, and got an uneasy bite to eat. Then we headed home, which was still another two hours away.

We got out of the car on the ferry ride across Lake Champlain. The air was warm, the breeze soothing. One large white bird flew in front of the boat, caught in the light for just a second. It was long-winged, silent and beautiful.

No cars were on the road. No lights were on in the houses we drove past. We were wide awake and totally exhausted at the same time.

We turned down our road, and drove the final three miles in silence until we saw our own house, right by the river where it was supposed to be, with the lights left on, in welcome. We stopped the car and opened the trunk to grab our luggage. Then slowly and care-fully, we opened the porch door, took a deep breath, and reached for the door knob of the front door of our home.

We crossed that threshold at 1:30 in the morning one full week after the bear's visit. It was finally time for us to see what the bear had done to our lives while we were gone.

Chapter 5

A Handful of Adirondack Poems:
Glimpses Through the Seasons

first light

at first the morning sunlight strikes
the tops of trees on the hill out back
all else is cold and nearly dark
but a robin is singing
so you know it's all about to begin

if you step outside
you shiver
and your breath fogs up around your nose
suddenly you hear another robin sing
somewhere down the road
then your robin answers
delighted not to be alone—
your fingertips are cold
this planet spins such a slow spin
you know the sun might not reach you
in time
to make your life worth living
to give you a shadow for companionship
to wash you in its forgiving, golden rays

there, now you see another tall tree
light up on another hill
smiling, tagged with love—
but the waiting down here in the river valley
is long and cold
and now you can't feel your fingertips anymore
and the cheery robins have their own job to do,
no matter what shiny hope you wanted to find
in their liquid sunrise song
on still another, all-too-familiar
cold and unforgiving morning
at the end of a long winter
that just wouldn't leave,
just would not
would not
make way
for spring

advice: about spring cleaning

When you are not a kid anymore,
when you clean your room after
a long time of dust gathering,
maybe on a cool spring day
when it rains and snows outside,
you learn something about your time,
about the order of things in a life

from experience you know
someone else will have to one day
sort the things in your attic,
the things in your room,
never guessing or giving a second thought
to your memories or passion—
tossing that note or photograph
into garbage somewhere,
along with crayon pictures your kids drew
when they were small, and the figures had circle faces—
someone else will take out the trash,
the walls will forget
and grow bare—
someday
that will come.

so now
as you clean your room,
and put another layer of your life
into a cardboard box for the attic,
touch those things
while they're still yours—
the coin pouch full of wheat pennies,
the incense from the sixties,
the baby's impossibly tiny undershirt,
the ring your grandmother gave you-
look at the pictures—
and remember taking them, that day, that angle of sun

it is, after all, exactly
what they are there for—
play old records, recall the words
and sing along—
remember who you used to be,
before
the dust settled in.

when Maurice broke his arm

On the other side of this hospital wall
I was keeping track for you—
Sitting in the sun by the river
the loudest sound was the twittering
of small birds-the gurgle of spring run-off
sung from deep wet pockets of joy.
I thought of you somewhere on a Potsdam sidewalk
with your sudden broken arm
and blinding pain, the deep hot flash
like a slap from a crazy, angry woman,
lingering, searing deep in your arm—
the memory of lying in the snow unable to move
waiting for help
not waiting to die, but maybe dying a little bit
hot tears running
down the side of your cold face.

Strange pillows, hot white room, no clothes
of your own, open hospital gown
letting your ass out
for all to admire—
the nurse wondered if you were homeless,
or if you had a job, not knowing
the expansiveness of your life
how many students you'd taught
or how famous you were—
It is so hard to be you right now,
in your prison of walls and smells, that
I brought some of your wild spirit
out here by the river—
In this sun your weathered face
grins like it used to,
is again at peace—
soaks up all that gurgling joy—

Breathe cool and deep right now
my friend. Take it slow.
The air is crisp and sweet
on the other side of this wall—
spring ice is melting, the river runs fast.
Just wait until you taste

how cool the water
is in this glass
in this sun.

Just you wait.

fishing: man and boy

The boy becomes a man
watching the men around him
shave in a mirror
shout at a game,
put gas in the car—
He learns courage
from comics and movies
and action heroes—
wanting to take a deep breath
that is just his,
a boy begins
with just one step—

The man becomes a father
with discomfort
at how much he does not know
about babies and small things
should he put his finger in the baby's mouth?
is it okay to let the child
sleep on his chest?
what if this small boy
hears him swear?
man spends years
trying to figure out what
is most important
to do with a child,
unsure of what to provide,
he fidgets the seasons away

When after some long thoughts,
the man finally shrugs,
taking a deep breath
that is just his,
he takes just one step—
he learns the day and time
of companionship—
no fear of bears or bad guys,
or dark-eyed enemies with guns, they are
trees together in the forest
rustling in the same wind
while life's curling river whispers below
waiting to be fished
by a man
with a boy by his side

raking

so it's the end of April
and I'm out raking
letting the rake's tines
sort through what is old and dead
and what is ready for the sun
I pull twigs and soggy leaves
away from pebbles and sand
I tug at wet brown grasses
knotted in the dreams of winter
my shoulders pull as I reach out,
lethargy lost to the wind.

my eyes sting, looking for a bright green sign
that everything alive did not die
in the heartlessness of a bitter winter
branches swipe at my face
brambles prick at my hands
and my back aches, almost longingly

I need to breathe air
not contained by walls,
I need to sort the remnants of winter
with an old rake,
I need to smell musk, damp earth,
and moving breezes,
and I need to hear
ducks whistling overhead
as they seek open waters
I need to feel the hot muscles in my arms
pulse with purpose—
I have earned this.

these basic needs are reasons why
at the end of April
I grip the old wooden handle,
blistering up my soft, dirty hands—
I'm out here raking my winter blues away, working up a sweat,
ignoring snow piles under the shadows,
brittle ice on puddles,
and the cold misty breath
clouding up around my face
blinding me to the truth

of sorrows still too hard and frozen
to be pulled away
by just this old rake
and these aching arms

no matter how hard I try

dreamcatcher

early morning, soft,
humid and gray—
a small breeze blows down the mountain
and the leaves on the trees
bend and bounce
early morning remembers the sweet dream
that woke you and brought you
downstairs to gaze out the window
small birds bend their heads
and grab seeds from the feeders
a hummingbird dips
his long beak into the red flower heads
one after another, sipping joy
flutter, dip, flutter, dip

so deeply quiet you are
as you hold tight to the dream
you hear a cat purr,
the hum of the refrigerator
and through the window
tiny songs of morning sung by
early birds who have only dreamt
these seeds, these bouncing branches
this new summer day

you know a dark storm is coming-
this warm wind,
these gray skies and low clouds—
being middle-aged and wise,
you've seen the signs before
and still
like the hummingbird
you dip back into your sweet dream
over and over again
sipping joy
before that summer storm
rising over the mountain
blows everything
away

lullaby

outside comes an even, pounding wind
filling all the forest, surrounding us—
if you must walk in it
you will be either helped
or hindered
in reaching your goal—
a forest wind is a steady engine
humming and pushing powerfully overhead—
with a sudden whoosh and shudder
sometimes branches crack, fall—
but mostly it's a steady rustling hum
dancing tree limbs, leaves like feathers—
a strong gust will scare you,
knock you off your mark,
push your hat off your head,
make you look around, worried—

when the trees' big boughs break
anything can happen,
they could fall on your car
or break the kitchen window
you might even die
if one hit you in the head—
you do not trust big wild wind—
pushing you around as it gives you unpredictable direction—
sometimes you just want to hide from it all

nothing is certain right here, either,
in this little closed room
where you write by a small light—
only out there in the whirling madness is the truth,
only when it rumbles and rustles deeply
banging on the house
gusting and charging,
do you know
your true mother's voice
rocking you, rocking you
in the treetops

to touch the wood

lifting pieces of wood off the ground
on a hot summer day
sweat drips on your cheeks, mats your hair—
your fingertips explode in joy—
if you know nothing else, you know that
you were born to touch these peeled trees,
these simple pieces of forest,
these golden jewels of local lumber yards

the length and heaviness stretch over
each board you heft—you find the center
while every movement tests your fingers, rolls your muscles
just as they were meant to roll, in a perfect life—
just as they did in all your other lives,
when you were a carpenter, a builder,
or maybe a caveman, gathering logs and branches
for the tribe, lifting, tugging, grabbing tight, carrying—
all true to the DNA in your coursing blood
now scabbed over on scratched and toughened hands
absentmindedly stroking the wood as you set it down again

in another life you were a handyman, someone I would be
glad to have stop in,
at ease with ideas for fixing broken things
possessing a clever way with hammer, saw and nails—
you understand the love of wood
and all that comes of it—
the steadiness of arm,
hammering nails, lifting planks—
the sensibility of measuring,
looking at the tape, writing down what you learned,
then checking once more—
seeing what hasn't yet been made
clear as right angles
and straight as the horizon—
feeling the warm sun on back and forearm,
moving through its day overhead,
creating shadow and substance with your help,
and the gifts from a dozen trees—
passing love on, with sweat and an easy grin,
your father to you, you to me—
the zing of the perfect strike,

steel hammerhead finding its target,
the soft powder feel of well-sanded edges,
the tight and true ring of a carpenter's saw—
you're standing back when the job's done, pencil behind your ear,
in your hands, an old broom for sweeping up the mess,
your heart full
with sympathy for the sweet smell of sawdust
happiness in the dependability of hammers,
and with a sacred and intense
lifelong
passion for pine—

Cider pressing in the Adirondacks:
"And apples, such sweet tart apples..."

August

chirping crickets
listen
can you hear them?
cheepcheepcheep— ·

the truth of August is
meteors tracing through dark night skies,
leaving trails of white mystery,
promising electric kisses—
fruit growing madly fills itself
with sweet liquid essence—
raspberries, blackberries,
juice dripping from summer lips—
sun so bright
air so sweet
families of birds gather, chatter,
frolic, and feed—
then disperse, in a flap of fearless feathers.

  our children, sensing truth with wide eyes,
  grow hungry for enough summer to last
  forever—
  nights begin to cool
  trees begin their orange tipped turn
  to autumn—some red leaves so bright
  they make you cry.
  empty schools in sleepy towns
  are cleaned, preparing for voices, elbows
  and jostling in large hallways
  and apples, oh, such sweet tart apples,
  and buttered corn on the cob...

  tingling
  with the greatest anticipation
  one brilliant
  red leaf
  falls right on your head
  crowning you king
  in the brightest sun—
  who sees this?
  somewhere a bear,
  somewhere else

a trout—and here,
perhaps a flock of robins
hopping on the grass.

August requires you
to drink of its fruits,
to know its name as sung by crickets at night,
to ready yourself for the next of your life,
to recognize the truth
when it is given to you,
and get on with this immense journey
you've just begun

songbirds, leaving

When the first leaves turn red,
at the very beginning
of the end of summer,
your heart races for a moment
thinking maybe notebooks must be bought
or a new pencil sharpened
somewhere close to you.

When green apples in the trees fill with roundness
and red stain blushes the tight skin
you know what "plenty" looks like,
your cheeks pucker in anticipation
of tangy juices dripping
from the corner of your smile.

When mist rises from the river
and fog hovers on every morning's road,
you feel the planet shift and tilt
away from mostly light
towards mostly dark—
a time of thinking hard thoughts
rises in this mist.

You must walk through a cloud, every fall.
Even when you do not remember
where the road takes you,
or where the edges are, the deep ravines,
slippery rocks, or waterfalls—
if you are to live, you always
must boldly walk
right into this autumn fog.

Letting go,
losing control,
saying goodbye,
knowing somewhere deep inside
the truth of this beginning,
the celebration of orange and red
falling leaves, tumbling, flying free
like songbirds leaving, like geese honking overhead.

A HANDFUL OF ADIRONDACK POEMS

In all this breathless golden glory
we see a darker truth—
Some must stay behind
and in the cold bleak winter time,
pause to remember
that first red leaf, the swirling mists
and the faces of those
who got away.

gold out here

mid to late afternoon,
I'd call it mid-autumn,
so it is essentially pure
gold out here—
back porch
half sun, half clouds,
blue sky in the middle of it all
an anxious river
full of fallen leaves
catching on round rocks
passing by me
along the way

midway through a life
I find sometimes noise
from this river is too loud
telling me more
than I need to know
getting to the ultimate end
much sooner
than necessary—
but there are other times
when the living bubbles lightly
carry me over broken glass
and brambles
when the song is rich and slow,
soothing the sliced edges of hard times—

mid way
between who I used to be
and who I will become,
some even spots on my face
will grow lines of explanation
some place under my eyes
will gather tears of goodbye—
it's about fifty out here right now
mid way between pretty cold and mighty hot
mid way between full and empty
middle of wonder, middle of pity
middle of awe,
all because it's so utterly,
luxuriously, purely and totally
gold out here

winter of '03

An ode to the sudden passage of the New York State Department
of Environmental Conservation deer-feeding ban

To keep the starving deer away
we built fences around the backyard
using what we had lying around—
elsewise they came and stared
into our windows while we watched television
or ate our supper—
you could see the glisten
in their dark eyes

There is a ladder and an overturned chair
propped by the back door and over there
two old doors, with white chipped paint,
positioned side by side,
and an end table
turned on end, in between—
I used an old Christmas tree
over there, by the fence,
standing crookedly in the snow—
Way off to the barn side
is still another old door,
laying on its side,
with a few screens from windows
we no longer have
propped up behind
held together
with tomato plant wire baskets
sticking up, like so much
razor wire, just without the slice—
all this doesn't matter—
the herds of deer still come—
every day they pass by
on their roaming tour of nothing-to-eat—
they walk up to these strange fences—
sometimes they keep walking,
slowly, and they stumble—
sometimes they jump
over it all—
they knock down the tomato baskets
they tip over the screens

they fall onto the propped up sideways doors
or try to crawl under them—
small deer, starving,
ribs showing under mottled winter fur
mother deer standing nearby
watching the next generation
disappear
before their dying eyes

Hungry deer on the deck

the plow

in memory of my father

snowplow ahead of her
on the lonely highway—
heavy metal monster pushing the cold, sloggy mess
with its massive iron blade,
curling snow up and off to one side of the road—
shooting sparks as iron strikes cement,
sand spitting out the back
giving her wheels something to hold on to—
today the job is wet and sluggish
another time, it will be blustery and white—
highway guys smoking cigarettes up there
playing country music in the cab
drinking coffee for the five ay-em shift—

This day, the plow trudges onward, steadfast
ahead of the girl
lights blinking red and yellow, a mantra,
it's okay, it's okay, kid—
she's going somewhere at a dangerous time
when maybe she shouldn't—
she is a little bit afraid
and she's hunched up behind the wheel—
wipers squeaking back and forth
back and forth—
Some comfort rides behind the plow, she thinks,
Some insurance, some strange, soggy security.
But man, there is some impatience.
So slow this going, so fast the heart.

But she has learned never to pass by
this kind winter savior, her guide, her umbilicus—
no matter how short her breaths
or how fast her heart—
she knows he may easily vanish up ahead
in a swirling cloud of white, blinking lights and all,
falling off the face of the earth—
leaving her on her own
on the slippery road
before day remembers
to rise up and take firm hold—

177

One day, she knows, this will come to pass—
So for now, just keep it in sight—kick back,
keep the window open a crack—
Blink, blink
do not cry
it's not time for that right now
just drive, honey, just drive

Christmas morning

is dark and cold.
I rise so early
that it is deep night.
I listen for Santa
as I've always done—
then taking a deep breath
I go downstairs
to see no presents under the quiet tree.
I put the kettle on for tea
and begin gathering wrapped gifts
from nooks and crannies
and put them carefully
in their spots under the balsam boughs.
I plug in the lights
and angels sing.
More and more trips
up and down the stairs
with dozens of colorful packages
all sizes and zesty with joy—
When I am finished
putting oranges and tiny gifts
in the stockings hanging by the fire,
I go out into the dark
and put birdseed around
for my feathered friends,
then I come in, and sit on the couch
with my tea cup balanced on my lap
I stare at the tree, blinking merrily.
The night outside the window
rolls undeniably to gray
then brighter and lighter
until those first birds come
happy with their gifts—
they are singing joy to me.
I thank Santa for coming
and wait patiently
with my tea
for the light in my children's eyes
to dazzle me
one more time
before I grow old.

memere's cross

outside the window
snow piles high—
all white out there, piled higher than the sill—
an empty page waits for the story

memere's black wooden cross sits
in this window,
Jesus hanging down
in my kitchen.
Used to be, the cross stood in her lonely room
and kept vigil with her and the lord at night.
Now she is gone, her room is gone
the holy water and rosary must have gone with her.

Here, now,
this crucifix stands dark against the bright snow—
I miss something about her,
some small quiet intake of breath
some tricks she knew about sewing torn shirts
darning socks, making meat pies, watching her soaps,
wearing hats with veils, and soft white gloves,
remembering the towering feel of high heels—
some solace she got from her lord
before he really let her down.
I think this cross in my kitchen
keeps her angel
restless—
we do not bow to it, or genuflect,
although we do our good deeds
and say we're sorry when we've done wrong—
I think she needs something more
before resting forever.
I intend maybe to go to church one of these days.
I want to tell her I am sorry
it all ended so badly—
then I will go deep into the woods, listen to the birds,
and walk quietly by the river
to say one of my prayers for her.

I keep this dark cross up for her dyed brown hair
covered with a flowered silk scarf, tied under her chin—
and her bright darting eyes and painted ruby lips—

for her longing for her youth—
for respectability and class—
and all the paths not chosen—
I keep some sacrifice in my heart
and catch a quiet breath
as I gaze out the window
past Jesus
into the deepening snow.

photo by Colin Surprenant

About the author

Randy Lewis has been living in the Adirondacks since 1972, moving to Saranac Lake right after an almost three year stint living in northern Germany. She is a poet and essayist, and an amateur naturalist, all reflected by the tone of the essays in *Actively Adirondack*. She now teaches writing part time at North Country Community College, and leads an Adirondack writer's group called Pen and Parchment. This diverse group of writers meets regularly, and performs often at readings in the area.

A former copy editor at the *Adirondack Daily Enterprise*, Randy loves words, both their grammatically correct and poetic usage. Among the places her poetry has been published are *Blueline*, *Many Moons*, the *Northern New Yorker*, and the *Paterson Literary Review*, where her poem "by the Oldsmobile" won honorable mention in the Alan Ginsberg National Poetry Contest in 2003. She is one of four poets appearing in *A North Country Quartet*, a book of northern poetry published by Potsdam College Press in 2006. Her essays, film reviews and features have appeared in the *Adirondack Daily Enterprise*, the *Lake Placid News*, the *Sequel*, and *Adirondack Life*. From 2000 to 2001, she was a writer and researcher for National Public Radio's *A Writer's Almanac*, where she also selected poems for the daily reading at the conclusion of this nationally recognized broadcast.

Among her hobbies are walking, swimming, birdwatching, traveling, reading poetry and practicing photography. A regular visitor to New York City, she enjoys immersing herself in urban culture regularly to enjoy its good ethnic cuisine and lively art.

She is the mother of three sons and wife of Neil Surprenant. After more than 25 years, they are still living in Paul Smiths, N.Y. next to the St. Regis River, in the shadow of St. Regis Mountain, watching the seasons change year by year.

Randy Lewis is available for readings and writing workshops. She may be contacted at activelyadirondack@roadrunner.com.